LET US PROPHESY

Let Us Prophesy

CHELSEA HAGEN

Copyright © 2025 by Daniel Hagen Ministries
www.danielhagenministries.com

First published, 2025 by Bekker Media for Daniel Hagen Ministries

All rights reserved. No part of this book may be reproduced in any manner whatsoever without written permission except in the case of brief quotations embodied in critical articles and reviews.

First Printing, 2025 by Ingram Spark

Printed by IngramSpark
ISBN: 978-0-6459220-0-4
ISBN Ebook: 978-0-6459220-1-1

Unless otherwise specified, all scripture taken from the New King James Version , Copyright 1982 by Thomas Nelson . Used by permission. All rights reserved.
Scriptures marked KJV are taken from the KING JAMES VERSION (KJV): KING JAMES VERSION, public domain

Cover design by Katherine Munro
Edited by Bekker Media

Contents

Dedication	v
Acknowledgements	vi
Endorsements	vii
Foreword	x
INTRODUCTION	1
1. One Moment Changed Everything	3
2. What Is Prophecy?	7
3. Who Can Prophesy?	13
4. The Purpose Of The Gift Of Prophecy	19
5. Hearing, Recognising, And Obeying God's Voice	31
6. Testimony - The Difference Between Life And Death	46
7. Communicating God's Heart	52
8. A Stranger's Voice We Will Not Follow	61
9. Calling Things That Are Not As Though They Are	70
10. Stepping Out To Prophesy	79
11. Testing A Prophetic Word	101
12. The Office Of A Prophet	107
Postscript	116
About the Author	117

This book is dedicated to Jesus Christ; without Him rescuing me from hell's gates none of these pages would ever have been written. I am forever grateful for my beloved Jesus.

Acknowledgements

A massive thanks to my precious family. My wonderful husband, Daniel, was not only instrumental in my salvation, but has always championed me in my walk with God. I greatly value and appreciate you.

My wonderful children, Reece, Esther, Caleb, and Abby, you are my pride and joy. You are the greatest gifts I could ever ask for. I am blessed beyond measure. Thank you for always believing in me and for your endless love and encouragement.

Thank you to Ben Fitzgerald for taking the time to write the foreword for this book and for being such a dear friend and blessing in my and my family's life. We are blessed to run alongside you.

A huge thank you to Beverly Bekker of Bekker Media for bringing this book's bones to life. Your encouragement and enthusiasm for getting it out to the masses have been invaluable. Thank you for your excellent editing skills and endless passion to see people's stories told.

A huge thank you to Kath Munro for your thoughtful, incredible, anointed artwork. I could not have imagined a more beautiful cover. I am delighted with it.

A huge thank you to each of you who have taken the time to read and endorse this book; you have all greatly inspired and impacted my life. Thank you for inspiring me to give it all to Jesus and to continue to run the race set before me.

Endorsements

Chelsea Hagen's book *Let Us Prophesy* is such a gift to the church and prophetic movement. A practical, rich, solid, deep guide to the wonderful workings and outworking of the prophetic. This book is written by someone who knows Jesus deeply, is a friend of God and walks in such purity and maturity in the prophetic. It will equip and empower you for the days ahead and help you dive deeper into an understanding of the Lord's heart for the prophetic.

Lana Vawser
Lana Vawser Ministries

Let Us Prophesy by our friend Chelsea Hagen is a comprehensive road map for real-life application of the prophetic in today's world. It doesn't shy away from covering all aspects of mature application, working within biblical truth and protocol, with user-friendly principles that unlock much needed discernment upgrades. Through relatable stories speaking to today's culture, you will receive balanced wisdom keys for the fruitful operation of the prophetic gifting, along with new passion to see people and nations transformed today.

Chelsea is a trusted and leading voice of revival and a soul-wining specialist. Her life is marked by fire, salvations, miracles and love for Jesus. This is not just a book to read, but fiery truth to add to your life, underline and refer to often. Grab it and let every page burn and brand your heart.

Jodie and Ben Hughes
Pour It Out Ministries

Chelsea Hagen brings clear and helpful insights on the role of prophets and prophecy in the church today. Speaking from a wealth of experience and a deep love for Christ and His church, Chelsea addresses important issues relating to prophetic ministry and discernment that will be a great help and encouragement to anyone wanting to grow in the prophetic.

With inspiring personal testimonies about the power of the prophetic, *Let Us Prophesy* will inspire and equip you to hear the voice of God.

Katherine Ruonala
Senior Leader Glory City Church, Founder and Facilitator of The Australian Prophetic Council

Chelsea Hagen is an amazing and passionate communicator, and her book *Let Us Prophesy* is jam-packed with great tools, instructions and testimonies to help you grow in your prophetic calling.

Let Us Prophesy will expand your capacity to hear the voice of God with clarity and will equip you with the insight and understanding to communicate what you hear with maturity and grace. Chelsea provides vital foundational keys in the prophetic, as well as steps to continued growth and development. This is a book that will inspire and provoke you to pursue a deeper relationship and intimacy with the Lord by hearing the 'still small voice' of the Holy Spirit saying, "This is the way; walk ye in it". *Let Us Prophesy* will stir your heart and add great value and purpose to your spiritual journey!

Prophetess Faylene Sparks
Director of Australian Company of Seers

Chelsea is a 'now' prophetic voice. In the many years I have known her, I can say without hesitation that she is unchanging, authentic, and on fire for Jesus and His truth. Through the trial years of Covid, I never once saw her waiver; she is steadfast and true. Her book, *Let Us Prophesy*, reflects this and I guarantee that you will not walk away unchanged after reading it. This book is a collection of teaching, stories and insights, passing on the torch of prophecy. So, light up your flames and let us prophesy over the nations in these last days!

Christy Johnston
Author of The Esther Mantle, The Deborah Mantle and Releasing Prophetic Solutions.

Foreword

I have known Chelsea Hagen since 2005, and within the first week of meeting her she shared with me prophetic impressions and was able to clearly articulate what God was showing her. Most importantly, they were coming to pass. Over the years I've only seen that grow, as well as her ability to help others do the same.

She is a person of great integrity and one of the most on-fire women I've ever known.

In *Let Us Prophesy,* Chelsea takes you through her journey as well as a sound, biblical dive right into the heart of prophecy and the prophetic ministry. She distinguishes the different ways God communicates His heart to us and how we are to then communicate that to others. What I really love about this book is that it shines light on the areas of prophecy that can be very vague. For example, Chelsea does an amazing job explaining the differences between the gift of prophecy and the office of a prophet in God's house. She also shows how to avoid false prophecy and hearing from the wrong spirit, and how to grow in discernment.

You will be greatly encouraged as you read this. It will give you many more keys and, most importantly, the passion to use your tongue as a vessel for God to touch the world.

I cannot recommend Chelsea Hagen and this book enough; read it with faith that God will ignite a fire in you for His Word.

Ben Fitzgerald
Senior Leader, Awakening Europe

INTRODUCTION

Thank you so much for taking the time to read this book. My hope is that you have picked it up because your heart yearns to know how to prophesy.

My aim in writing this book is to accelerate your understanding of the prophetic, both Biblically and practically, as well as cover the difference between the office of a prophet and a prophetic gifting.

In my many years of ministry I have come across numerous Christians who are confused and unsure about whether God is truly speaking to them. I have heard them ask questions like:

'How do I hear the voice of God?'

'Does God want to talk to me?'

'How do I learn how to hear His voice?'

I want this book to be a simple yet powerful kick-start to your prophetic journey with the Lord, so that you too can be confident that God wants to talk to you. I share many lessons that took me decades to learn, and I believe this information will help to short-cut your journey in the prophetic.

God greatly desires for you to prophesy.

In simple terms to prophesy means to convey the Father's heart, His will and intentions for an individual or group or nation.

I wrote this book to encourage you that you too can hear, recognise and obey the voice of God. It is not just for a chosen few but for every single born again believer. We are created to have a covenant love relationship with God. Imagine that after marrying the love of your life, moving in together and sharing the same house, you never speak to each other. That would be weird and unnatural. It would be a non-existent relationship. Yet so often our relationship with God can be like that. He lives inside of us, and He yearns to communicate with us, His beloved. He desires relationship above all else. It has always been God's will that every person can hear His voice and prophesy.

By the end of this book, I believe you will be confident to recognise, hear, and obey God's voice.

Chapter 1

One Moment Changed Everything

Chapter outline:

> ◦ The power of a single moment in the prophetic journey.
> ◦ Setting the stage for exploring the prophetic and its significance in our lives.

I love the transforming power of true prophetic ministry. My life was personally and powerfully impacted by a minister who stopped in the middle of a church service to prophesy over me. I had never met her before, yet she knew intimate details of my life that only God could have known. She prophesied over me for forty minutes. This powerful demonstration of the prophetic gift drew me into such a radical encounter with Jesus; one that I am still marked by today.

This encounter was a pivotal moment in my life. At this point in my life, I was an alcoholic, although I would never have admitted it back then. I couldn't go a day without a drink; my body would shake in the morning because I needed one. I was also on a high dose of antidepressants as my life was dominated by extreme fear and panic attacks; I was constantly suicidal and couldn't wait to get off this stupid planet. My life was on the wide path of destruction with one broken relationship following another. I was steeped in gross sin, which was all an outward symptom of a very broken little girl trying to do life without her God.

If God did not step in when He did, I believe I would be in hell right now.

This was a crossroads in my journey where I was confronted with the reality of the Gospel. This powerful prophetic gift in action completely changed the course of, not only my life, but my generational line. This is why I am so passionate about the power of one prophetic word.

As a result of this encounter, I immediately realised that Jesus Christ was alive and well and very real. I could never, ever again deny His existence.

As I sobbed my heart out before Him, He showed me my life. Nothing was hidden from Him - every single motivation of my heart, every action, every word was laid bare and exposed.

He showed me that things I did that I thought were good in my eyes were wrongly motivated by selfishness. He showed me all the times He had desperately tried to reach and rescue me, and all the times I had callously rejected Him.

The realisation of the filthiness of my life in contrast to a holy and beautiful God was all too much for me. I knew that He was just. I knew that He was right, and I felt so horribly ashamed before Him. I tried to back away from Him. I was absolutely not worthy to bask in any of His magnificent glory.

I so desperately wanted Jesus to get away from me. I knew with every inch of my being that I was a wretched, dirty, rotten sinner before God. The more I tried to back away from Jesus, the more love came, the more compassion came, the more mercy came. I just completely broke under the conviction and power of the Holy Spirit. True repentance came and I wept bitterly. In that moment I promised to serve God every single day of my life, no matter what it cost me. I promised Him I would never, ever let Him go.

I realised Jesus was nothing like people had said. He was more beautiful than I could ever have imagined.

It is hard to describe what I experienced that day; words seem so inadequate to describe the presence of Jesus. I have no yard stick on this earth big enough to measure that kind of love. I wept like a baby, sobbing uncontrollably at His feet. Never have I experienced such love. His mercy and compassion have changed me from the inside out and marked me forever.

As I lay on the floor with tears pouring down my face, my life a completely shattered mess, little did I know the journey that lay ahead of me. Little did I know the wonderful restorative and redemptive work that God would weave through my broken life.

I had no idea in that moment, on the 28th of February 2004, how much my life would be changed and utterly transformed for God's glory. Everything changed in one moment in His glorious presence: just one moment of meeting my precious Saviour. I knew that I was standing on the threshold of a brand-new life with Jesus. My mind was made up - I would follow Him every day of my life.

I am now even more in love with Him. To this day I can't even think about that time without tearing up.

God is no respecter of persons; what He has done for me He wants to do for you. The Bible says that when we seek God with all our heart, we will find him.

'And you will seek Me and find Me, when you search for Me with all your heart.' (Jeremiah 29:13)

On the prophetic journey, we often underestimate the profound impact that a single moment can have. The Scriptures remind us of the power inherent in moments when the secrets of the heart are revealed. 1 Corinthians 14:24-25 states, '*But if all prophesy, and an unbeliever or an uninformed person comes in, he is convinced by all, he is convicted by all. And thus, the secrets of his heart are revealed; and so, falling down on his face, he will worship God and report that God is truly among you.*' In these transformative moments, when prophecy operates authentically, it can expose the hidden thoughts and intentions of the heart. This divine revelation, occurring in just a moment, can trigger transformation, conviction, and redemption. It is in these powerful moments, as God unveils the depths of our souls, that lives are forever changed, destinies are altered, and individuals are drawn closer to the heart of God. Such moments in the prophetic journey serve as powerful reminders of the extraordinary impact that one encounter with God can have on our lives and the lives of those around us. Do not ever underestimate the power of a single prophetic word in one divine moment.

Reflecting on the immense impact of that one prophetic moment in my journey, emphasises why it is so important for us to gain a deeper understanding of the prophetic and why it matters in our lives. This moment clearly demonstrates what is described in 1 Corinthians 14:24-25 - hidden thoughts are exposed. To learn how this can become a reality in our lives, we will explore how we can hear God's voice, grasp His intentions, and witness life-altering transformations through prophecy.

In the chapters ahead, we will uncover who has the ability to prophesy, the purpose behind this divine gift, and how it plays a vital role in our personal relationship with God and its potential impact on the lives of those around us. I encourage you to continue reading with a teachable heart and an open mind, understanding that one prophetic moment holds the power to change everything.

Chapter 2

What Is Prophecy?

Chapter outline:

> - The Biblical concept of prophecy in the Old and New Testaments.
> - A personal testimony to demonstrate the role of prophecy.
> - The role of the prophetic gift in the context of the church today.

Defining Prophecy in Biblical Terms

Prophecy, in biblical terms, is the communication of God's heart, emotions, and divine intentions on specific matters. This divine inspiration accurately conveys God's will. An example of this is found in 2 Peter 1:20-21, *'No prophecy of Scripture is of any private interpretation, for prophecy never came by the will of man, but holy men of God spoke as they were moved by the Holy Spirit.'* This passage highlights the divine origin and purpose of prophecy to convey God's truth to humanity. We see this demonstrated all through the Old and the New Testament. God communicated with people in many different ways through people, writing, visions, dreams, trances, and angels. He used prophets to bring a message about His will and desires, which encouraged people, but also brought warnings and correction to people, cities, and nations.

The Differences between Old and New Testament Prophecy

Throughout the Bible, we observe changes in the expression of prophecy. In the Old Testament, prophecy often involved foretelling future events, such as the prophecies of Isaiah about the Messiah's coming (Isaiah 7:14). In contrast, New Testament prophecy expanded to include edification, exhortation, and comfort to build up believers.

1 Corinthians 14:3 speaks of prophecy as a gift that *'speaks edification and exhortation and comfort to men.'*

Let me share an example of a prophetic word that greatly encouraged my husband Daniel and I during a particularly challenging time. I vividly recall Daniel having a dream which was a message from God that would be profoundly encouraging to us in the days and months to come. Before I fell pregnant with my third child, God told Daniel in this dream that I would fall pregnant soon with a little girl and that we were to call her Abigail. We found out later that Abigail means 'Fathers joy' in Hebrew. The dream was quite simple; God said, "Everything will be okay in the pregnancy and the birth and after."

Well, the word in the dream did not make one hundred percent sense at the time, but sure enough, shortly afterwards I fell pregnant with a little girl. During the course of the pregnancy, I developed some blood clots and the birth was an emergency caesarean section, which we had not expected. Five hours after Abigail was born the doctors discovered a growth in her throat. As we were in a little hospital in Nambour, Queensland, they did not have the facilities or the right equipment to help her. So, they bundled up my brand-new baby and took her via helicopter to Brisbane. They would not let me go with her as I had just had a caesarean and was not physically able to make the trip at that point.

As our little daughter was being whisked away in the helicopter, Daniel was driving down to Brisbane by himself, which is about an hour's drive away. Not only did I not have my baby with me, but I also did not have my husband with me either. I recall feeling robbed of a time that was meant to be a great celebration. I remember looking at my baby girl with little headphones on her ears being bundled up by the nurses ready to go in the helicopter, feeling so awful about being separated from her. In the midst of all that turmoil and fear, however, I remembered what God had spoken in that dream, "everything will be okay, through the pregnancy, the birth and after." It brought me great comfort in that really tough time. It was then, and only then, that I had a full understanding of why God had given Daniel that dream and said those few simple words.

In that moment of helplessness and separation, God's promise served as an unshakeable anchor for our faith. Our faith was not in vain, for God's word held true. The journey was challenging, but in the end our little girl, Abigail, emerged as a living testament to God's faithfulness. Everything was indeed okay, just as He had promised us.

This remarkable experience deepened our understanding of the purpose of prophetic words. They are not without purpose; they are lifelines of hope and assurance, guiding us through the most trying of circumstances. Our journey with this pregnancy and birth was marked by uncertainty, but God's promise held us steady. It was a reminder that even in the darkest moments, His words are a light to our path and bring comfort to our hearts.

Exploring the Various Forms of Prophecy in the Bible

There are diverse forms of prophecy in the Bible. For example, there are the prophetic visions and dreams experienced by Joseph which foretold his rise to power and the future of Egypt (Genesis 37:5-10). Another form is direct communication with prophets, as seen in the encounters between God and Moses (Exodus 3:1-10), or Elijah on Mount Carmel (1 Kings 18). Additionally, apocalyptic visions like those in the book of Daniel, provide profound insights into future events.

The Prophetic Role in the Context of the Church Today

In the New Testament, after Jesus' resurrection and ascension, He established structure within His Church and bestowed gifts upon it, including prophets (Ephesians 4:11). This illustrates that prophecy is an essential part of the Church's life. Prophets, such as Agabus in Acts 11:27-30, played a vital role in conveying God's specific guidance and revelations. The Church is meant to be a unified body in which each part, including prophets, contributes to the spiritual growth and well-being of believers.

While prophecy is a powerful gift from God, it should never replace the Bible, the infallible Word of God. Prophecy serves as a valuable tool for encouragement, guidance, and comfort, but it must always align with, and complement, the authoritative canon of Scripture. God's Word is unchanging, and prophecy operates within the bounds of God's timeless truth. As we continue to explore prophecy, we will discover its profound impact on our faith journey.

What is a prophet?

A prophet is one who receives a message from God and speaks it to another. (Acts 3:18)

A prophet is a messenger for the King, a spokesperson from Heaven, an ambassador who accurately represents God's word and His heart and Kingdom on earth.

The first thing that Jesus did after He died and rose again was take back the keys of hell and death, then He established structure and order within His church – He gave gifts to men.

Ephesians 4:8-13, *'Therefore He says: "When He ascended on high, He led captivity captive, And gave gifts to men. (Now this, "He ascended"—what does it mean but that He also first descended into the lower parts of the earth? He who descended is also the One who ascended far above all the heavens, that He might fill all things.)*

And He Himself gave some to be apostles, some prophets, some evangelists, and some pastors and teachers, for the equipping of the saints for the work of ministry, for the edifying of the body of Christ, till we all come to the unity of the faith and of the knowledge of the Son of God, to a perfect man, to the measure of the stature of the fullness of Christ.'

Prophets are one of God's gifts to the church; they are one part of the five-fold ministry (apostles, prophets, evangelists, pastors, and teachers). Prophets were never meant to operate on their own, as lone rangers apart from the Body of Christ. They were given to operate as part of a team; every gift we have been given is to be used in conjunction with being planted and submitted to authority within a local church body. No single person carries all revelation - we need each other. There is no room for pride – prophets are only one part of five. We must remember we all see dimly now, until we meet Jesus Christ face to face.

To illustrate, imagine a bottle of water in the of middle of a table and five people sitting around that table. If I asked them what they could see, each person would give me a different answer. One would say, 'I see a barcode', one would say, 'It's a blue label', another, 'I see writing', another the brand name. They are all looking at the same bottle, but they are seeing different aspects of it. Apostles, prophets, evangelists, pastors, and teachers are not meant to argue and be divided over what they see, but rather understand that each gift enables that person to see a different part that is highlighted to them. The important thing to remember is that each office sees in part. By working together in unity, we can see a fuller, clearer picture.

A prophetic word is never, ever meant to take the place of the Bible, the infallible word of God in the canon of Scripture. What we hear and speak in the prophetic is not canon Scripture because we already have that, and we are not meant to add or take away from Scripture.

God's glorious word is forever settled in the heavens. Psalm 119:89, *'Forever, O Lord, Your word is settled in heaven.'*

Chapter 3

Who Can Prophesy?

Chapter outline:

> - Addressing common misconceptions about who can operate in the prophetic.
> - Highlighting the inclusivity of the prophetic gift.
> - Encouragement for every believer to engage in prophetic ministry.
> - Practical examples of where and how to practice prophetic ministry.

Spiritual Gifts

Anyone who is born again and baptised in the Holy Spirit can operate in all nine gifts of the Holy Spirit. 1 Corinthians 12:4 -11, *'There are diversities of gifts, but the same Spirit. There are differences of ministries, but the same Lord. And there are diversities of activities, but it is the same God who works all in all. But the manifestation of the Spirit is given to each one for the profit of all: for to one is given the word of wisdom through the Spirit, to another the word of knowledge through the same Spirit, to another faith by the same Spirit, to another gifts of healings by the same Spirit, to another the working of miracles, to another prophecy, to another discerning of spirits, to another different kinds of tongues, to another the interpretation of tongues. But one and the same Spirit works all these things, distributing to each one individually as He wills.'*

The nine gifts are as follows:

1. the word of knowledge,
2. the word of wisdom,
3. the gift of prophecy,
4. the gift of faith,
5. the gifts of healings,
6. the working of miracles,
7. the discerning of spirits,
8. various kinds of Tongues, and
9. the interpretation of Tongues.

When I was first born again, I thought I had to ask God separately for each gift, not realising that once I was baptised in the Holy Spirit and spoke in tongues, I already had access to all nine gifts. I spent a lot of time asking God for what He had already so generously lavished upon me. I didn't understand at the time, that the passage of Scripture that led me to that conclusion was actually talking about the operation of the gifts of the Spirit in the context of a church meeting.

Of course, not everyone in the church can share a word in the one meeting - it would take too much time to have a word from every single person in the congregation. Not everyone in the church can pray for healing in one service. Why? Because nothing else would get done. God has created you to prophesy; you may not get an opportunity in a Church service, but outside of the church service you can most certainly lay hands on the sick and prophesy; there is a pulpit on every street corner – so go for it! Prophecy needs practice, practice, practice.

Putting God's Word into Practice

I would often hit the streets and ask people if they would like a word of encouragement. Most people were incredibly open to that, but I would get the odd one that would tell me to get lost. As I practiced, I would get more and more accurate details about people from God. At other times I would completely miss the mark and slink off in the opposite direction, embarrassed and hoping I would never see them again.

If we do not practice, we will not grow, so even though I was scared I would make myself have a go.

We need both the hits and the misses to improve, finding out in the process whether we heard from God or not. I remember the enemy trying to discourage me so much when I would miss it; he would torment me about how I am a failure, and so I would give up.

Can I encourage you that no one on this planet starts off as an expert at anything. It is through learning, perseverance, mistakes and failures that we grow the most. Everyone has to start somewhere, so go for it!

I would simply ask God, "Lord, what is one thing about this person that I can say to them that would help them know that You are real?" He would show me a picture, or a few words that would be relevant to them.

On one occasion I remember God said that I was to take a lady's shopping trolley back to its allocated spot for her. She asked me "Why would you do that"? I said, "Because Jesus loves you so much, He wants to help you." Immediately, as soon as I said that, I knew she was suicidal. I told her that God did not want her to take her own life, and she just broke down and wept.

She had been planning to take her own life that very night. She ended up giving her life to Jesus Christ! This wonderful ending was as a result of me simply offering to take her trolley back, as the Lord had instructed me. Prophesying does not need to be complicated; you do not need to bust and strain for a word for someone. Just ask God, "How can I show Your love to this person in front of me today?"

God showed me information that in the natural I could not possibly know, but God knows, and He cares. Jesus came to seek and save that which is lost; He seeks out those who are hurting and broken.

The gift of prophecy can be like a tap - you first need to turn it on and run it for a few minutes to get it flowing properly. That is what happened with this lady – I opened the tap by offering to take her trolley back and then God gave me a revelation about her suicidal thoughts while we were having a conversation.

Is that not wonderful news - that you are already able to access and function in the gift of prophecy; it is for every believer!

The way that we develop and get stronger in the gifts is by simply exercising them - putting them into practice. There is no point having the word and not actually doing it. If we are just hearers of the word, it will not benefit us at all. In fact, the Bible says we are deceived if we are not putting God's word into action. (James 1:22)

It's like going to the beach on a hot summer's day and leaving the sunscreen in the glove compartment. Sunscreen is no good sitting in the glove compartment! You actually need to apply it for it to work. Without application you will get sunburnt. The word of God is the same, you need to apply it and keep reapplying it to get the full benefit.

As the Bible says in Romans 10:17, *'So then faith comes by hearing, and hearing by the word of God.'*

The way that we grow in maturity is by doing what the word of God says.

Whenever we learn something new, it can seem clunky and uncoordinated at first, but with a bit of persistence and perseverance we grow. The more you practice anything, the easier it becomes and before you know it, it will become second nature to you.

I started by practicing the gift of prophecy on people in the supermarket or at the petrol station. I would ask them if they wanted a word of encouragement. I figured that if I got it wrong, I would never see them again anyway! Honestly, you cannot go wrong when you encourage someone; everyone needs encouragement.

There were plenty of times I fumbled and stumbled over my words at the start. I felt very awkward, uncomfortable, and downright fearful, but I made myself step out of my comfort zone and the more I practiced and stepped out, the more I realised that I did not need to worry. I had an expert with me - the wonderful Holy Spirit! He is always willing to reveal things about people so that they come to realise and understand that Jesus Christ is real.

One of the funny stories I will share with you is about one night when I was out witnessing and prophesying. Because I was so nervous and new at having a go, I jumped straight in and did not even bother to first greet one poor person. There was no idle chit chat either. I had just felt like God had revealed to me that they had liver problems. So, I thought, "Okay, I will just step out of my comfort zone and share that with them." Because I was so nervous I just asked them straight out, "Do you have liver problems?"

Well, how terrifying for them! A girl randomly emerges out of the shadows to ask them about their liver. Needless to say, they were freaked out and walked away very quickly. No wonder!!! The poor person has probably never gotten over the shock. I still laugh about that to this day. I am convinced God has a blooper reel in Heaven and the cloud of witnesses have a good laugh watching us. Of course, this is just my imagination!

You do not need to be weird when approaching someone to prophesy - just be yourself. Talk, have a chit chat, have a laugh with the person. I promise you the more you practice, the easier it will become. Just be yourself; that is when the anointing will flow the best.

Chapter 4

The Purpose Of The Gift Of Prophecy

Chapter outline:

> - Understanding the primary purposes of prophecy as revealed in Scripture.
> - Prophecy as a tool for edification, exhortation, and comfort.
> - The role of prophecy in spiritual growth and building community.
> - Discerning God's specific purposes for your prophetic gift.
> - Discerning God's timing.

What is the Primary Purpose of the Gift of Prophecy?

The primary purpose of the gift of prophecy is that people may know how much God loves and cares for them and this knowledge will draw them into a relationship with Jesus.

1 Corinthians 14:3, *'But He who prophesies speaks to men to edification building, confirmation) and exhortation (consolation, comfort, entreaty) and comfort.'*

Let us have a closer look at what those words mean:
Edification - build up, encourage, lift up.
Exhortation - to come alongside, to strengthen.
Comfort - love, comfort, God's presence to touch that person.

1 Corinthians 14:1-4 and 12, *'Pursue love, and desire spiritual gifts, but especially that you may prophesy. For he who speaks in a tongue does not speak to men but to God, for no one understands him; however, in the spirit he speaks mysteries. But he who prophesies speaks edification and exhortation and comfort to men. He who speaks in a tongue edifies himself, but he who prophesies edifies the church.'* And verse 12, *'Even so you, since you are zealous for spiritual gifts, let it be for the edification of the church that you seek to excel.'*

That word *excel* in the koine Greek, Strong's G4052 *perisseuo* - to super-abound in quality and quantity, increase, be in excess of.

The Bible tells us in 1 Corinthians 14:39, *'Therefore brethren earnestly desire to prophesy.'*

And in 1 Corinthians 14:1 *'....and desire spiritual gifts, but especially that you may prophesy.'*

Also, in 1 Thessalonians 5:20-21, *'Do not despise prophecies. Test all things; hold fast what is good.'*

Knowing God's Heart

The only way that you are going to truly know God's voice is by knowing and understanding His character - who He is and who He is not. We must know His heart and intentions, and one of the ways we understand these things is by reading the Bible, the precious Scriptures.

So how do we know when it is God's voice? I will explain it this way: let us say you receive a text message on your mobile phone and there is no emoticon added. You could read the message and misunderstand it completely if you are not familiar with the person who sent it. The message could be understood in various ways - like the person is angry, sad, annoyed, having a joke, or being serious. If you do not know the heart of the person sending the message it can very easily be misconstrued and taken out of context.

If I know the person and understand their heart, I will receive the text the right way.

So, it is with the Bible. Unless I understand the Author's heart behind the text, the message He is trying to convey can easily be misconstrued, taken out of context, and be understood completely differently to what was originally intended. If, however, I know God's heart I will understand the Biblical text and receive the message as it was originally intended.

John 1:1, *'In the beginning was the Word, and the Word was with God, and the Word was God.'*

And John 1:14, *'And the Word became flesh and dwelt among us, and we beheld His glory, the glory as of the only begotten of the Father, full of grace and truth.'*

Jesus is the Word of God made flesh and is the exact representation of the nature and character of the Father. When we read all the things He said and did as recorded for us in the four Gospels, we will have a clear understanding of the nature and character of God, our Creator, and what His intentions are toward us.

The key to hearing our Creator accurately is found in the precious words of John 15:4-5, *'Abide in me, and I in you, As the branch cannot bear fruit of itself, except it abide in the vine, no more can you, except you abide in me. I am the vine; you are the branches. He that abide in me, and I in him, the same brings forth much fruit, for without Me you can DO NOTHING!' (emphasis added)*

The more time you spend with someone the more you really get to know them. God is not looking for a surface, superficial relationship. He deeply desires a true relationship with each one of us. We can truly bare our hearts before our King who deeply loves us through the good, the bad and the ugly, no masks required. This relationship is a safe place where we are mouldable and pliable in the hands of our Potter. We must bow our knee to God's will, purposes, and plans - Christianity is about denying ourselves and following Him.

When we are in love with Jesus and seek intimacy with Him, our hearts will want His will to be done. The Bible says in John 14:15, *"If you love Me, keep My commandments."'*

His commands are not grievous.

We do not seek God with the wrong motivation – just to improve in a gift. We seek God purely because of who He is. This puts us in a place where our hearts, having been touched by God, are so grateful and thankful and in love with Him that we will want others to know that He is real.

There is nothing wrong with wanting to operate in the prophetic gifting as long as we keep our hearts and motives pure. We are never to elevate the gift above Jesus. The purpose of any of the gifts is to draw people closer to King Jesus, not to draw people to us. The goal of the gift is that people would know that Jesus Christ is real and that we give them an opportunity to be reconciled to the Father through Jesus Christ.

The purpose of the gift is to show them that Jesus knows them, sees them, and hears them. We do not want to just 'wow" them with the gift but give them an opportunity to be born again and start their journey of being a disciple of Christ.

Everything we do should be done from a place of close intimacy with Jesus, from that place of love. Otherwise, we can end up misrepresenting Him. The gifts are not given to us to make us look good or to pump up our egos, but to always glorify and magnify Jesus Christ. To Him alone belongs the glory. Our goal must never be more ministry opportunities; that will naturally happen when we set our attention and affection on God. He must always remain first in our lives; we must be completely captivated by Him and understand that He is our source.

We must remember that we do not have anything that He has not given us. There is no room for pride in the Kingdom of God. Pride is ugly and self-righteousness is even worse. Let us remain full of humility when operating in the gift of prophecy.

Identity

It is imperative as a Christian that we are able to hear God's voice. We were created to hear His voice and to be in a relationship with the Lord. We have at some point chosen to follow Jesus, but here is the thing - how do we follow Jesus if we cannot hear Him? How will we know which way to go if there is no two-way communication with our King? God created us for relationship, to have conversations with Him, to intimately know Him and love Him. In other words, understanding our identity and who we are in Christ is crucial to being able to accurately capture God's heart for a person when we prophesy.

The Bible tells us in 2 Corinthians 5:17, *'Therefore, if anyone is in Christ, he is a new creation; old things have passed away; behold, all things have become new.'*

We have been born again; a brand-new creation! The thing is, even though our spirit has been made perfect, God does not give us amnesia or a lobotomy. The majority of the time we still think and feel the same way we did before we were born again.

What we need is to renew our minds. We need a new hard drive, so to speak; the old one is obsolete and will not take us extremely far. The Bible shows us that we are transformed by the renewing of our minds. Romans 12:2, *'And do not be conformed to this world, but be transformed by the renewing of your mind, that you may prove what is that good and acceptable and perfect will of God.'*

Isn't that amazing that the Greek word for transform (*metamorphis*) is the same as a caterpillar turning into a butterfly. We are literally transformed into something completely different by reading the word of God and putting into practice. We are changed from the inside out to reflect the nature and character of God.

Check out some of the amazing inheritances you have now obtained. In just the first two chapters of Ephesians the Bible tells us:

- We have been blessed with every spiritual blessing.
- He chose you in Him before the foundation of the world to be holy and blameless.
- He has adopted you.
- You have been redesigned for the pleasure of His will.
- You are accepted in the beloved.
- You have been redeemed.
- You have been forgiven by the riches of His grace.
- You have an inheritance in Him.
- He loves you with great love.
- He is rich in mercy.
- You are alive in Christ.
- He is exceedingly kind towards you.
- You are seated in heavenly places.
- You have been brought near by the blood of Jesus.

- You are no longer a stranger but a member of the household of God.
- Christ is our peace.
- We have been reconciled to the Father.

I would encourage you to go through those chapters and beyond and underline them, or colour them in in your Bible; write them down somewhere, memorise them, mediate on them, and remember who you are in Him. Do not let the enemy trick you out of your inheritance. Hold fast to what He says about you. One of the things that God challenged me on was that, when I doubted what God says about me, I am actually calling God a liar. I am putting His character on trial.

It would be like you telling one of your children over and over, "I love you." And showing them through your actions that you love them, but despite all this, they keep saying, "No you don't." You repeatedly try and express to them just how much you love them, repeatedly saying, "Yes I do." But they keep saying, "No you don't!" They simply do not believe you. That would hurt the heart of any parent and so it is with God. We MUST take Him at His word!! Do not waiver in believing His love for you. It is written and God's word will never, ever change. Be secure in His unfailing character.

You are a son or a daughter of God. You have been adopted into the Beloved; you have come out of the kingdom of darkness into His glorious light. He knows every hair on your head. He lovingly knit you together in your mother's womb. He knows when you lie down and when you sit up. God places value and honour on every one of His creations.

Unless we understand how much God loves us, that He loves us as He loves His Son, Jesus, we will not be able to accurately prophesy God's love over others. Being able to see the way God sees, is paramount to the prophetic. This includes the way we love and see ourselves.

Jesus is better than I could ever have imagined. There are not enough pages in the world to accurately describe His wonder and stunning beauty. Yes, it has been a journey and yes, I have had to hold on through the good, the bad and the ugly, but I have already made up my mind - God has my continual 'yes', no matter how hard the road looks ahead. I have met and fallen in love with my Beloved and there is no turning back. We have to be in it for the long haul; we have to be doers of the word in all aspects of our Christian walk. If we are persistent and persevere, we will see change and transformation.

Prophetic Words and Discovering Our True Purpose

Prophetic ministry was a major turning point in my life, one that I am eternally grateful for and one that caused me to continually pursue love Himself. Getting to know Jesus has kept me strong for the race set before me. The prophetic is so powerful when you have that understanding that God sees and hears everything you have ever said or done or thought, and yet He still loves you. He died for us while we were yet sinners. WE were the joy set before Him when He died on the cross.

He has been with you through the best of times and has known when you have soaked your pillow with tears alone at night. He is so desperate to reach His lost kids; He is always trying to communicate and show Himself to be real. Jesus knows how to reach each individual heart. He never stops trying. He pursued me and continues to pursue me with relentless love. Our relationship with the Lord should be the greatest love story ever told. Just like a good marriage, we should be more in love at the end than in the beginning - mature love that has weathered storms and yet stood firm because of His greatness.

Can I encourage you today - pursue this gift God wants you to have. He wants to impact and change lives just like He crashed into my life in 2004 when I was so broken and so messed up that I didn't think God could make anything beautiful out of my life.

He has done over and above, more than I could have ever hoped, or dreamed. He has restored and reconciled my true purpose, which was to worship and live in communion and fellowship with Jesus. He has lavishly poured out His love and kindness for which I am eternally grateful. And, as I said before, He is no respecter of persons - what He does for one, He will do for another. He wants to transform your life!!! In every area!!!

There are so many men and women, boys and girls out there who, like me, desperately need to hear His sweet voice, who desperately need to know He is real, and who desperately need hope to cling onto. So, I pray that as we continue working our way through this book, you too would be able to easily recognise His voice and share His heart and His great love and compassion with others.

Every gift that God gives to us is to always be a signpost to lead people into a personal encounter with God. We show people the gift and introduce them to the Gift Giver.

A Word of Warning

It is a powerful and life-changing gift to draw others closer to God. Unfortunately, like any authentic gift, there is always a counterfeit. The prophetic gift has frequently been misused. One thing we are seeing is the rise of so-called prophets calling out false, although accurate, words of knowledge. These false prophets, prior to attending a conference or service, will get the names of those attending and look up some of their profiles on Facebook. They then use that information to identify those people in the service, pretending that the Holy Spirit has supernaturally imparted the information to them! This is wicked and must be stopped. God will not be mocked!

We will further explore false prophets and true prophets in chapter eight.

There are definitely authentic prophetic gifts and words of knowledge, and as with anything, you don't throw the baby out with the bathwater - you just learn to spit out the bones as you discern what is of God and what is not. Once we recognise God's voice, we cannot unrecognise it. God tells us not to despise prophecy, but rather to test all things.

At times, in extreme cases, an unhealthy reliance on man is created when people will constantly go to a person operating in the prophetic gift, instead of going to God for themselves.

At the other extremity are those who despise prophetic words and miss what God is highlighting in a particular season.

It is a wonderful, powerful gift and I have seen many lives changed and transformed by it, but like in all things, we do need to have a healthy balance - test the word and do not hang your life on a person's prophecy, but rather put your full trust and your full hope in God. A prophetic word is not the infallible word of God, only the Bible is one hundred percent accurate and infallible and will never fail you. Do not place the same weight on a prophetic word if it is not canon Scripture. Just because someone prophesies it, does not mean it is absolutely accurate. It is going through a fallible human filter.

We must remember that we all only see dimly until we see Jesus face to face.

Another thing to remember is that a prophetic word speaks to the persons potential. Its fulfilment is conditional on our obedience to follow Jesus on the narrow path. It won't just happen without our partnership and co-labouring with Jesus. The prophetic is like an invitation - God invites you to something better in your life, something you have not seen in your life. He reveals His purposes and plans that He dreamt over you before you were in your mother's womb.

Let me give you an example, so that I can explain myself a little better.

Let us take the world's best athlete. They are not born the best athlete in the world. Yes, they certainly have the potential and are given the opportunity, but it is through consistent practice and exercise that their potential comes to pass.

An athlete's body is not going to get fit all by itself sitting on the couch eating doughnuts. You get what I mean – fulfilment of prophetic words requires a partnership with the Lord.

It also requires a great amount of sacrifice and commitment and dedication to become the world's best athlete. There is a time of preparation and sacrifice along the journey. In the same way, God may have given you a dream over your life and has graced you to do it, but that does not mean that you are automatically going to fulfil it. There must be intention and focus on your part to see it come to pass.

God is Never in a Hurry

One thing I have noticed over the years about God is that He is never in a hurry. God is not a fast builder. He is a thorough builder, which takes time. God may give you a word and you may not see it fulfilled until twenty years later.

Take a look at the life of Joseph in the Bible. God gave him a dream and then he was falsely accused and imprisoned. Yet, what seemed like a setback was actually Joseph's springboard to His next victory. God was training and equipping him for something far greater than himself, but he needed to be tested first in the small things - in his faithfulness, in his endurance to keep believing against all odds. His character was being developed over those thirteen years. When God shows us something over someone's life, it does not mean it is going to happen next week. It might take ten years or longer before you see something happen.

The only thing that tests authentic prophecy is time.

As you wait for your prophetic words to be fulfilled, be faithful and steadfast where God has planted you. Be a blessing to your leadership, teachable, and humble, serving God faithfully with a can-do attitude. God will get you to where you need to go.

Hebrews 13:17, *'Obey them that have the rule over you, and submit yourselves: for they watch for your souls, as they that must give account, that they may do it with joy, and not with grief: for that is unprofitable for you.'*

Don't despise the day of small beginnings - from little things big things grow.

The Bible says we need to wage war with our prophetic words. Write them down, read them, believe them; prepare in any way that you can, to see them come to pass. We will explore this further in chapter ten.

1 Timothy 1:18, *'This charge I commit to you, son Timothy, according to the prophecies previously made concerning you, that by them you may wage the good warfare,'*

Chapter 5

Hearing, Recognising, And Obeying God's Voice

Chapter outline:

- Developing spiritual sensitivity to God's voice.
- Discerning the difference between your thoughts and God's voice
- The importance of obedience in prophetic ministry.
- Practical tips for recognising when God is speaking.

Let's begin with a list of some of the ways God speaks:

- Through His word (He will NEVER contradict His word, and does not make exceptions)
- Audibly
- Prayer
- Praise

- Music
- Holy Spirit
- Prompting/impressions
- Small, still voice
- Dreams
- Trances
- Angelic
- Visions
- Books
- Through people
- Nature (Psalm 19:1-2, 'The heavens declare the glory of God; And the firmament shows His handiwork. Day unto day utters speech, And night unto night reveals knowledge.')
- Language of the spirit
- Art
- Open eye vision
- Dance
- Tracts
- Encounters
- Miracles

The second one I mentioned is audibly - I have heard God's audible voice many times in my life, but the very first time brought about an amazing miracle.

I had just been born again, but was still smoking and drinking in the pubs. No-one told me I should not have been drinking, and even if they had I would not have listened. I was still a work in progress, learning who I was in Christ. Before being born again, I would need to drink every single day and, as I said earlier, towards the end would be shaking in the morning because I needed a drink. Looking back, I realise I was definitely an alcoholic, although, as I said, at that time I would never have admitted it.

I remember this as if it happened yesterday. It was St. Patrick's Day, 2005, and I was in a little country pub in a place called Bunyip in Victoria, Australia, affectionately known as the Middle of Nowhere. At that point, I had already consumed seven beers, which was remarkable for me, as normally I would drink until I dropped. In my world there was no such thing as having just one beer; I simply did not see the point of that! It was there, in the middle of nowhere, that I heard the audible voice of God. He said, "Do not forsake me." I knew it was the Lord, and a holy fear of God hit me straight away, penetrating to the core of my being. I put down my drink and have not had one since that moment.

That was almost twenty years ago, at the time of writing. Not only did God deliver me from alcoholism, but He also ripped the root of it out of my life. From that time onwards, I have had an intense hatred of alcohol; I cannot even stand the smell of it, or the thought of it, and I cannot even eat alcohol in cooking. Only God has the power to do that. I had no withdrawal symptoms, no longing for or needing alcohol. It was an absolute miracle.

I made a covenant with God that I would never touch alcohol again. I was so grateful and thankful to be supernaturally delivered from this subtle demon in a bottle, which had sought to destroy my life.

God is always more than willing to help us, always making a way where there is no way. We get ourselves into some really difficult places, but God is the Almighty Deliverer. I did not even ask Him. He just crashed into my world.

God can deliver us from these addictions, but we must choose never to go back.

Ephesians 5:18, *'And do not be drunk with wine, in which is dissipation; but be filled with the Spirit,'*

I have learnt that we cannot compartmentalise our walk with God. We need to be aware that He is very present 24/7, wherever we go. I heard His audible voice in a pub!

Discerning the Difference Between Your Thoughts and God's Voice

I hear so many of God's children discouraged that God does not talk to them and they feel that He does not want to. Or they are confused and not sure if it is truly God, or not. These are all questions I battled with when I was first born again. Is it God? Isn't it God? How do I know the difference?

I was so confused, and we all know that confusion is never from God. In the early days I really struggled, and I could never just step out in true confidence. I would feel double-minded and unsure of God's voice. But once I learnt to recognise His voice, I became confident and bold to declare His truth and His heart. So, my heart and the aim of this book is that you too can know the voice of God and step out in greater boldness and faith.

God's word says in John 10:4-5, *'And when he brings out his own sheep, he goes before them; and the sheep follow him, for they know his voice. Yet they will by no means follow a stranger, but will flee from him, for they do not know the voice of strangers.'*

Did you know you were created to be able to hear and respond to the voice of God? It is God's greatest delight to communicate with His children. He deeply desires a relationship with us; it is the one thing that God emphasises over and over in Scripture. He adores you and has always desired an intimate relationship with each one of us, without exception.

He cannot wait to spend time with you, walk with you, talk with you, hear what is on your heart, and share with you what is on His. We see this truth displayed right in the beginning of the Bible, in Genesis, where God is walking and talking with

Adam in the garden of Eden. When Adam was hiding from Him, God asked him, "Adam, where are you?" As if God did not know where he was! What He was doing was creating space for communication.

Nothing has changed. He still desires two-way communication with His children.

God is not some far off, aloof, disengaged God shouting orders from Heaven. Rather, He wants to be near to us, to be deeply involved in every aspect of our lives. He sent His Son, Jesus, to die so that we could have a relationship with Him, so that we could be reconciled to the Father. It was expedient for Jesus to depart so that we could have the Holy Spirit, the Comforter, here on earth. His desire is that we would commune with the Holy Spirit. He said He will never leave us and never forsake us; there are no exceptions. He is in it for the long haul. He is always available and willing, and His door is never shut.

The Bible says in Hebrews 4:16, *'Let us therefore come boldly to the throne of grace, that we may obtain mercy and find grace to help in time of need.'* It does not say knock and take a ticket and get in line. We can freely come to our Papa and He is always willing to help.

Words of Knowledge

Words of knowledge are a way of supernaturally knowing something that is currently true in someone's life.

The way that God taught me to move in words of knowledge, something that I had no prior knowledge of, started like this: I would be in church, and I would feel a phantom pain in, for example, my left wrist. I would think, "Well, that's strange. My wrist wasn't hurting before."

At the end of the service, during the time of ministry and prayer, someone would come up and ask me to pray for their left wrist because they had injured it. It took me a few times to understand that this was the way that God was trying to speak to me. He was showing me their pain, so I knew exactly how to pray for them.

God reveals supernatural information to us so that others can be set free. God is a God of great compassion and mercy, and Jesus paid a heavy price so that we could be set free from all pain, sickness, and diseases. It is His great desire to heal us physically and spiritually.

Now, because I have learnt to recognise and understand the way God speaks to me, and I exercise the gift, it is like second nature. I know exactly what I need to do when I feel a phantom pain in my body. As we practice not just listening to the voice of the Lord, but just as importantly, obeying what He is saying even when we feel fearful or are afraid, the easier it will become. Just step out and have a go!

There is no greater joy than seeing others free from pain and torment. It is truly wonderful!

Recognising God's Voice - Random thoughts or God's voice?

The Holy Spirit is very practical, and He always helps us if we invite Him into our everyday moments.

Shopping

Has this ever happened to you before - you are in the supermarket, and you get a thought that you need some rice (or something else)? You immediately start reasoning in your mind, "No, I am sure I still have half a bag in the pantry." Mentally you go through your pantry shelves, finally deciding, "No it's okay, I have plenty left over."

When this happened to me, thinking it was just my own thoughts, I did not buy the rice. When I got home, lo and behold - there was no rice! And I could not make the dinner I had gone to the supermarket to buy groceries for. The Holy Spirit is very practical. He was trying to help me because He knew I would have no dinner.

So often I have heard His voice in this way, but I have not recognised it as the voice of God trying to help me; instead, I just thought they were my own thoughts.

Roadworks

Another time, while I was learning how to recognise the voice of God many years ago, I was driving in my little Hyundai hatchback on a very hot day, when I had a thought, "Don't go the way you normally go as there are roadworks there. You will be stuck in the hot sun for ages."

Not realising it was the Holy Spirit trying to speak to me, I immediately started reasoning in my mind, "No, I always go that way. There weren't any road works there the other day."

I drove down the road, and sure enough I was stuck in traffic for well over an hour in the boiling hot sun. What made matters worse was that one of the car windows was broken and wouldn't wind down. My car would also regularly overheat, so I would have to turn the heater on full blast to bring the temperature down. I had sweat pouring off my head and felt like I was about to catch on fire. While I was waiting, I replayed that voice that had told me not to go down that road, and then I clicked, "Ahhhh ... that was you God! You were trying to help me bypass this whole, unpleasant experience."

The Holy Spirit was teaching me how to hear and recognise His voice. It was not that I did not hear what He was saying. I heard Him alright, but I thought they were just random thoughts or my own thoughts. So, the problem was not hearing His voice, but recognising that it was Him. After this experience I began to recognise His voice more often than not.

It is not a matter of just hearing and recognising His voice, but then also obeying what He is saying that is important when it comes to prophecy. Had I known His voice back then, I would have known not to go down that way regardless of what I thought to be true about the roadworks. So often we reason ourselves out of obeying when God is trying to help us.

Thoughts about people

What about this one - when you are at home, and you randomly think of a person. "I should give them a call," or "I should send them some flowers." You might think these are just random thoughts, but it is the Holy Spirit who knows that someone is needing encouragement or needs help with something.

He is trying to prompt you to respond. The Holy Spirit is funny; it is as if He is tugging on your coat trying to get your attention. If you do not respond or recognise that it is Him talking, He will keep tugging at your coat more frequently. Eventually, if we don't respond, He will try to get the attention of another believer until He gets a response so that the person who needs help, gets it.

Radical obedience blesses the heart of God. He knows He can trust you to get His will done on the Earth.

Later, after responding to the tugging of the Holy Spirit, you might hear from that person that something had happened or they were feeling distressed at that time, and then you remember, "Oh, that was the time the Holy Spirit prompted me to call them."

The Holy Spirit is always talking to us if we are tuned in and listening. God wants to get His will, plans and purposes done on the Earth, and guess what - He needs your hands and feet and voice to do it. He chooses to co-labour with us. That is why we must not just hear His voice but be obedient and quick to respond to be His hands and feet on the earth. We will unpack this a bit more in the next section.

Passport

Later on, when I had become more familiar with the Holy Spirit's promptings (the voice of God), there was a time when my husband was being picked up from our church by a minibus for a mission's trip. I was on my way to church to drop off his suitcase, when I heard the Holy Spirit say ever so clearly, "Daniel doesn't have his passport." I joked with Him and said, "You could have told me that twenty minutes ago, before I left."

He said, "You didn't ask." Fair enough, I did not ask!

So, I quickly drove back home, picked up the passport and got it to Daniel in the nick of time. It would have been a disaster for him to have arrived at the airport only to discover that he had no passport. It would have been too late for me to get it to him by then.

I wonder how many needless situations would be averted in our lives if we listened intently to the voice of the Holy Spirit. His is a still, small voice and it is very easy to override what He is saying with our emotions, with our own agendas and wanting to do things our own way.

Even delays are not always problems. They can be God's way of preventing you from having an accident on the road. Sometimes one minute can make all the difference. I have often been rushing, bemoaning the fact that I had left a minute or two late, but then passed an accident that had obviously happened just a minute or two before I arrived on the scene. I remember thinking, "I could have been in the middle of that."

Nowadays, I always ask Him, "Have I forgotten anything?" and I give Him an opportunity to speak. I invite Him into my everyday moments; He is an amazing friend, available 24/7 and always willing to help us.

> Can you remember a time like the ones presented here when the Holy Spirit was talking to you, but you haven't recognised that is was Him?

It is wonderful to be able to hear, recognise and discern God's voice. It is equally important to grow in maturity and actively obey God's voice. I love the story of how Mary, the mother of Jesus, knowing that obeying the voice of God can have miraculous outcomes, encourages the servants at a wedding to do whatever He told them:

'On the third day there was a wedding in Cana of Galilee, and the mother of Jesus was there. Now both Jesus and His disciples were invited to the wedding. And when they ran out of wine, the mother of Jesus said to Him, "They have no wine." Jesus said to her, "Woman, what does your concern have to do with Me? My hour has not yet come." His mother said to the servants, "Whatever He says to you, do it." Now there were set there six water pots of stone, according to the manner of purification of the Jews, containing twenty or thirty gallons apiece. Jesus said to them, "Fill the water pots with water." And they filled them up to the brim. And He said to them, "Draw some out now, and take it to the master of the feast." And they took it. When the master of the feast had tasted the water that was made wine and did not know where it came from (but the servants who had drawn the water knew), the master of the feast called the bridegroom. And he said to him, "Every man at the beginning sets out the good wine, and when the guests have well drunk, then the inferior. You have kept the good wine until now!" (John 2:1-10)

Great advice from Mary the mother of Jesus "Whatever He says, do it." This passage shows us that Jesus required the servants to act on what He said. They filled the water pots to the brim and Jesus turned the water into wine. We are all called to co-labour with God to prophesy and continue to bring about God's will on the earth.

The Tone of God's Voice

'But he who enters by the door is the shepherd of the sheep. To him the doorkeeper opens, and the sheep hear his voice; and he calls his own sheep by name and leads them out. And when he brings out his own sheep, he goes before them; and the sheep follow him, for they know his voice.' (John 10:2-4)

In Strong's concordance, the word in this passage for 'voice' is talking about tone - 'phōnē (fo-nay') - akin to G5316 through the idea of disclosure; a tone (articulate, bestial, or artificial); by implication, an address (for any purpose), saying or language: - noise, sound, voice.'

We need to know God's tone to hear His voice. A simple way of knowing God's tone is this: the devil is bad, and God is good.

Verse 5 in the passage above says, *'Yet they will by no means follow a stranger, but will flee from him, for they do not know the voice of strangers.'*

A word study of the original Greek of the words stranger, follow, and flee is as follows:

A stranger - αλλότριος (allotrios, pronounced al-lot'-ree-os), from G243; another is, that is, not one's own; by extension foreign, not akin, hostile: - alien, (an-) other (man's, men's), strange (-r).

Follow - akoloutheō (pronounced ak-ol-oo-theh'-o), from G1 (as a particle of union) and κέλευθος keleuthos (a road); properly to be in the same way with, that is, to accompany (specifically as a disciple): - follow, reach.

Flee - pheugō (pronounced fyoo'-go), apparently, a primary verb; to run away (literally or figuratively); by implication to shun; by analogy to vanish: - escape, flee (away).

So, in these we see that the stranger's voice, the enemy, has a different tone to the true Shepherd's voice. It is hostile towards God. We must be able to discern the difference - even the enemy masquerades as an angel of light.

One of the ways a bank teller knows if a note is a counterfeit or not, is they are taught to handle and to know a real note – what it looks like and feels like - its texture and weight. They hold it up to the light and check for the watermarks to know if it is genuine or not. It is the same with hearing God's voice - we want to look for the 'watermarks' of God's character. A prophetic word must be undergirded by His character, heart, and tone - this is how we begin to recognise the difference between God's voice and the stranger's.

What is God's character and tone like?

These are just some of the amazing, unchanging characteristics of God. I encourage you to take a moment to read through these characteristics of our incredible Creator.

He is Good - There is no shadow of turning in Him.

He is all truth, generous, the shepherd of our souls.

God is love, full of compassion, patient, holy, pure, our deliverer, a righteous and just Judge, powerful, creator.

He is goodness and severity, long-suffering, full of joy, patient and never changes. He is kind to the thankful and the unthankful, not tempted by sin, caring; He sends rain on the just and the unjust. He is humble, creative, stoops down to make us great, takes away our sin, compassionate, abounding in mercy, Prince of peace, defender, very present help in time of trouble, protector, abounding in mercy, slow to anger, and redemptive by nature. He is restorative, forgiving, gentle, a servant, faithful, loyal, persistent, never gives up, never fails us, and courageous,

He is tender-hearted, rescues us, cares about us, loves us; builds up, encouraging, defender of the weak; He corrects us, brings comfort, carried our sorrows and griefs, mourns with those who mourn, healer and great physician. He chastises us, provides for us, prunes us, changes us, transforms us, warns us, rebukes us, and is unwavering, unshakeable, steadfast, immovable, helpful and honest. He is a truth-teller and grace giver. He admonishes, is sinless, jealous over us, gentle, meek, mild, understanding, listens, hears us and wants to respond.

He is our strong tower, crowns us with loving kindness and tender mercies, available, approachable, convicts us of sin, friendly, lifter of our head and He knows us. It is not His will that any should perish, He never forces us to do anything, He respects and gives us our free will, He extends an invitation for us to come up higher. The goodness of God leads us to repentance. He is all knowing and omnipotent. He is Lord, supreme authority, a man of war and He holds all things together.

Let's looks at the tone of the enemy's voice (the stranger)

Bad - hostile, harsh, offers no solution or help to the problems, critical, condemning.

Unforgiving, despair, hopelessness, pushy, legalistic, tears down, causes doubt.

Confusion, unloving, dishonouring, controlling, manipulating, lording over.

Takes away choice, controlling and angry.

Discouraging, bitter, fearful, anxious, overbearing, self-righteous, quick to anger, masquerades as an angel of light, twists and perverts the word of God, hates you, abusive, depressing, self-hatred, condescending, curses, devalues, wants to bring forth death, torment, destruction, always tells you who you are not, liar, father of all lies, deceiver, distorter of the truth, full of pride, tempter, unholy, murderer, causes offense, bitter, jealous, brings disunity, arguments, fights, brings for death, sin, false, keeps things in the dark, hidden, disobedient, stubborn, wicked, disguises himself, opposes God, prowls around seeking who he can devour, blinds the minds of the unbeliever, rebellious. Enemy of God, accuser of the brethren, schemer, comes to kill, steal, and destroy, foreign, hostile.

So, as we can see, based on these Biblical descriptions of God and Satan, there is an enormous difference in their tone of voice - they are polar opposites.

Once we recognise God's tone, we will not be fooled or deceived into listening to or following the voice of a stranger (the enemy).

Activity

Do you honestly believe that you can have an intimate relationship and communion with God?
If not, what do you think some of those blockages could be?
How well do you feel you currently hear from God? (rate from 1-10)
Write down one time where you have heard the voice of God.
List one way you recognise God's voice.
How has God spoken to you?
How do you know that it is God?
What are the clear markers that it is God?
How do I know when it is not God talking to me?
List three characteristics/tones of the good shepherd.
List three characteristics/tones of the stranger.

Activation

What is He saying to you personally? Take 10-15 minutes to write a prophetic word from God over your own life. Ask Him things like "How do you see me? What are you doing in this season?"

Chapter 6

Testimony - The Difference Between Life And Death

Chapter outline:

> - A compelling real-life testimony illustrating the life-saving power of prophecy.
> - Reflecting on the impact of prophecy on critical life decisions.
> - Emphasising the life-transforming potential of the prophetic gift.

God teaches us and trains us to hear His voice because sometimes being able to hear His voice is the difference between life and death.

I share this story with you to inspire you and to illustrate just how important it is to recognise God's voice, to be able to hear clearly and then to obey.

In 2007, I was booking a flight to go to Queensland. I had already picked the date I was returning, but God said, "No, you need to leave the day before that."

"Honestly," I thought, "what difference does one day make?"

Nevertheless, I obeyed God and chose one day earlier for my return date, and thought nothing more about it.

About seven months prior to that God had given me a prophetic word for a friend - that she was going to fall pregnant with a baby girl. She was so delighted as she had been asking God for twenty years for a little girl. I had no idea about this. Sure enough, three months later she fell pregnant with a baby girl.

So, back to my trip to Queensland - I came back a day earlier as God had told me to do. I had a great sleep and the very second I opened my eyes, I heard the Lord very strongly telling me I needed to go to my friend's house. "Right now!"

I fumbled around for my phone, thinking I would just call her when I heard the Holy Spirit say again, "Just get in the car and go there. There is no time." I got in the car, not understanding what was going on, and proceeded to drive the forty minutes to her house. She was about twenty-three weeks pregnant at this time.

Much to her surprise, I turned up on her doorstep and said to her, "The Lord has told me to come. Is everything okay?" She seemed fine. She shared that she was in a small amount of discomfort which is pretty normal, being pregnant. She told me she was a little worried that her daughter was in a breech position. I said, "That's easy for Dad to fix." and proceeded to pray for God to turn the baby around.

I thought, "This is so weird God. I am sure you did not send me all the way here just for this."

We were sitting talking while she ate breakfast, and I heard the Holy Spirit say, "You need to get her to a hospital right now."

My friend assured me, "No, I am fine. I will wait until my husband gets home." Again, I heard the same from the Holy Spirit, "You need to get to her hospital right now," but in a more urgent tone. My friend was so stubborn, and I tell you it was no easy feat getting her into the car!

I finally got her in the car by saying I would take her to the doctor for a check-up. I did try to take her to her doctor, but she couldn't get an appointment as he was fully booked. The Holy Spirit kept saying to me, "You need to get her to a hospital." I kept going despite her protests and drove her straight to the hospital. The Lord's voice was louder than her protests. She was mortified!

I had no idea what I was doing. I was just following God's voice. Nothing appeared to be wrong. I just told her, "Come on. It can't hurt to get a quick check up."

When they did an examination on her, they discovered that the umbilical cord, which feeds the baby, had torn away from the womb and her baby was actually drowning in blood! The doctors immediately transferred her to another, better equipped hospital via ambulance for an emergency caesarean to try and save the baby's life. I was shocked at the events unfolding before my eyes.

Sometimes we do not need to know all the details of why God has asked us to do something, we just need to hear His voice and obey.

My friend haemorrhaged while having the emergency caesarean and lost a life-threatening amount of blood. Now both of their lives were in danger. My friend had the rarest blood type, O-positive, and they could not find any blood in supply in Victoria. I got a group of us to pray, and we kept praying and praying. Then, all of a sudden out of nowhere, a nurse came bursting in saying, "We have some bloods!" This was miraculous provision, and my friend could be given an emergency blood transfusion.

Miracle after miracle was unfolding before my eyes.

It is funny when you step out in obedience - sometimes we do not even understand the magnitude of the importance of hearing from God and obeying what He tells us to do.

The doctors said that had I got there twenty minutes later, the baby would have died.

I remember being so shocked to hear that. I finally understood the urgency of the Holy Spirit's voice earlier that morning. And the reason why God needed me to change the date to arrive home one day earlier from my trip to Queensland. Again, I didn't need to know all the details of why God told me to do that, but it was a matter of life and death that I obeyed Him.

I remember seeing this tiny little baby girl in her humidicrib weighing a total of 900g. This perfect, tiny baby girl that God had spoken to me about all those months ago.

They were not allowed to pick her up as she was too fragile. It was still touch and go for many months, her survival hanging in the balance as she was so premature. I prayed and prayed over her and said, "God, you told me to prophesy about this little baby girl." I declared, "You have a future and a hope for her." I kept declaring over and over and over, "You will live and not die in Jesus' name." She remained in hospital for two and a half months.

They both recovered, thanks to God's urgent intervention and they called this little girl Blessing, born in January, 2007.

Never underestimate the importance and significance of learning to hear God's voice in the smallest of things, because sometimes it does become about life or death. God could call you, as He did me, to stand in the gap for someone. Two precious lives were on the line and God saved both of them. I hate to imagine what could have happened if I had not obeyed the first step, which was to change the date of my flight with the travel agent.

Sometimes we have no idea why God is telling us things; it unfolds as we are obedient and even weak in our faith.

God also speaks to us in the ordinary, everyday moments. The amount of times we are actually flowing in the prophetic during everyday conversations, not even realising it, would surprise you. Has anyone ever said to you as you are chatting, "Funny you should say that. I was just thinking about that last night"?

Just be yourself and the prophetic will flow.

Activation

So, go for it! You can start today. If you are still struggling to approach someone, the best way to start is to do what I did:

Ask God to put someone on your heart and ask Him for a word for them. You can text it to them, call them, or simply write a card. I noticed that after doing this for a while, the accuracy and details of the words I received from God improved greatly, and so many people were encouraged and built up when I did this.

Chapter 7

Communicating God's Heart

Chapter outline:

> - The prophetic as a means of revealing God's heart – His thoughts and feelings toward us.
> - How prophecy can convey God's love, compassion, and desires for individuals.
> - Practical insights into delivering prophetic words that reflect God's character.

Stewarding God's Heart With Integrity And Honesty

Jeremiah 23:21-22, *'I have not sent these prophets, yet they ran: I have not spoken to them, yet they prophesied. But if they had stood in my counsel, and had caused my people to hear my words, then they should have turned them from their evil way, and from the evil of their doings.'*

In the last days, God warns us, there will be many false prophets that rise up. In this passage God is saying that He did not send or speak to these prophets, and yet they ran of their own accord. But if they had stood in His counsel, He would have spoken to them. God's desire for the true prophet is that they warn people of the wrath to come and to turn away from evil. Here we see prophets are to warn people when they go off the narrow path.

'And the Word became flesh and dwelt among us, and we beheld His glory, the glory as of the only begotten of the Father, full of grace and truth.' (John 1:14)

Good stewardship is being able to carry God's heart with the truth. We need to be a people who impart the full counsel of God. We never want to make things up; these things may sound good and appealing to the flesh but are of little or no benefit to the hearer. We must be a people that enquire of God and be prepared to wait on Him for the word of the Lord, the hammer that breaks apart the rock. We need to be people who lean into God and ask Him what He sees over a person, what He wants to say and how He wants to say it. Our job is to convey that word that God has given us with purity, honesty, and integrity, staying true to God's heart. We must remember we are just the messenger. We are His messengers on the earth, we are His hands and His feet, we are carriers of Heaven's glory to be poured out on others.

We never want to presume what God will say, we need to ask Him and wait for His response. We do not want to add what we think onto the end of God's response; just let it be as unfiltered as you can - straight from the source. When we steward God's heart, we say only what He is saying and do only what He is doing. Jesus said, "I only do what I see the Father doing." We must be the same. We cannot just run off when we get more practiced in the gift of prophecy, thinking we have got it all and can leave God out of the process.

When we are faithful with the words He gives us, then I believe God will begin to share things with us that are close to His heart. Over the years I have developed a history of trust with God - He knows I will not twist His words or the heart of His message. As you embark on your prophetic journey you also will develop a trust relationship with God.

Remember it is when we are faithful in the small things that He trusts us with more.

When we multiply what He has already given us, He will trust us to steward more.

One of the things I have learnt is that there is no point asking for more if I am not already using and practising what I have been given and is readily available. Unless I use it and practice, it will lie dormant and bear no fruit.

You have the Spirit of God living on the inside of you; the Bible says He withholds no good thing from those who love Him. He has given us every spiritual blessing in Christ.

'Blessed be the God and Father of our Lord Jesus Christ, who has blessed us with every spiritual blessing in the heavenly places in Christ.' (Ephesians 1:3)

I remember when I was first born again and being frustrated as I was reading about all these amazing miracles in the Bible – the deaf hearing, the lame walking, the blind seeing, and I said to God, "Why aren't I seeing these things?" His response (gosh, I love Jesus), "Well how many have you prayed for?" Good response!

You see, at that point I was not praying for any of those things. I was not exercising my faith and stepping out and praying for those ailments. Once I started stepping out of my comfort zone and praying for people, I saw many miracles. Again, I say - we must be doers of the word, not just hearers. The only way you get better at anything is by practice and more practice, learning from your mistakes, and more practice, commitment, and persevering through discouragement, staying the course until you see breakthrough.

Do not let the enemy knock you off track, stay focused and determined to learn and grow.

There are no short cuts in the Kingdom; you learn by doing.

Prophecy Reveals God's Heart and Moves Us Closer to Him

Put simply, the prophetic is being able to accurately relay a message from God with His tone and heart to individuals, churches, regions, or nations.

God's heart is always a heart of reconciliation and restoration. God's great desire from before the foundation of the world, was to reconcile man back to Himself in Jesus Christ. He is redemptive by nature. The prophetic is about stewarding God's heart and representing Him well by accurately communicating His heart and tone in what He is saying.

The true prophetic will cause someone to be more aware of God's presence and will move the person's heart one step closer to Jesus. Perhaps that person is a non-believer, and they do not want to hear it or acknowledge that Jesus is real, but we must always remember the seed that you plant is powerful. God will bring the increase; He will keep sending people to reach that person by any means possible. Before I was born again, I lived on Emmanuel Drive. If that is not a sign right in my face, then I do not know what is! God pursues us over and over again. So, don't be discouraged if you do not see any immediate fruit; just be obedient to what God is asking you to do in that moment.

The most important thing is that we just need to be willing to step out of our comfort zones, allow God to stretch us and be available, surrendered vessels for God to use. You do not need to be an expert; the Holy Spirit already is. When you step out, you will be surprised by how much He wants to reach people. God is always extending an invitation for us to come in deeper. He is calling us and beckoning us to draw near to Him and He will draw near to us.

God is a merciful God. The Bible says that while we were yet sinners, Christ died for us. When we prophesy over a person, we need to remember the value that God places on that individual; they are priceless and a valued treasure that Jesus paid for with His blood.

It is never a light thing to speak into someone's life, it is a privilege and an honour.

If we are saying we believe our prophetic words are from God, then we had better make sure that they carry His heart and love for that person.

The words spoken should be saturated in hope and truth. Even if that person is far from God, we need to lean in to see God's purposes and plans over that person's life, and call forth those things that are not, as though they are (see chapter 9).

Worship Jesus Christ Alone

'Then he said to me, "Write: 'Blessed are those who are called to the marriage supper of the Lamb!'" And he said to me, "These are the true sayings of God." And I fell at his feet to worship him. But he said to me, "See that you do not do that! I am your fellow servant, and of your brethren who have the testimony of Jesus. Worship God! For the testimony of Jesus is the spirit of prophecy."' (Revelation 19:9-10)

In this scripture, John the Revelator falls down to worship a fellow servant who brings a message of truth. The fellow servant tells him not to do that, but to worship God alone.

Let this be a lesson to us all as we grow in our prophetic gifting: don't make the mistake of worshipping the one giving the prophecy, and don't let people worship you because you flow in a gift. We are to continually give Jesus Christ all the glory and all the praise; we are to worship Jesus Christ alone and always keep Him at the centre.

As prophetic people, we don't want to just display the gift. We always want to use it to point people to Jesus Christ; our greatest mission on the earth is still the great commission.

'And He said to them, "Go into all the world and preach the gospel to every creature. He who believes and is baptised will be saved; but he who does not believe will be condemned.' (Mark 16:15-16)

Use every opportunity you can to lead people to Jesus Christ. Revealing Jesus Christ must be front and centre of all prophecy. Giving people a chance to give their lives to Jesus Christ and be saved from an eternity in hell should always be our primary mission.

It is not God's will that ANY should perish. Not even one.

Here is a practical example of what that could look like:

Once you have given a prophetic word, the person (who is a pre-believer at the time) might say, "How do you know that about me?" At this point, you have their full attention, like a deer in the headlights, so to speak; use that opportunity to try and then lead them to Jesus Christ.

My response "I don't know that, but I am a Christian, and Jesus revealed that to me because He knows everything about you and wants you to know that He loves you and is real. He died on the cross for all your sin and shame. The Bible says we have all fallen short of the glory of God. The wages of sin is death, but the gift of God is eternal life. Even though we are guilty and deserve the penalty of death, Jesus, in His great love and mercy, paid the price for you in full with His blood on the cross so that you could be reconciled to God the Father through Him. You need to repent and be sorry for your sins and ask Jesus for forgiveness for all your sins. Confess with your mouth that Jesus is

Lord, turn away from sin and turn to the living God so you can be saved and go to heaven."

Then take it one step further, "Is there any reason you wouldn't give your life to Jesus today"?

I have seen many people give their lives to Jesus on the spot. But even if they don't give their lives right then and there, you have planted a seed of the incorruptible word of God and God will bring the increase.

Present God's Solutions

It does not take a prophet to see and point out the problems in someone's life, but when we sense something is amiss, we must also present God's solutions. There is always a way out with God, there is always hope, always room for change.

Even if there are problems and difficulties in a person's life, God only sees the possibilities. He does not see anything as impossible. He is the eternal optimist. He will speak with correction, but He will always have a solution. There is always a way out with God, through repentance of sin and turning back to Him.

Love never fails; you can never love, encourage, or build someone up too much, especially when you are starting out in the prophetic. Everyone loves a word of encouragement; it is those little words along the way on the journey of life that people can hang onto, knowing that God has not forgotten them, that He is right there on the journey with them.

Sometimes God shows me that He simply wants me to pray for a person and not say anything. Don't feel that you have to have a word for every single person; sometimes during prayer ministry the Lord is wanting to minister to a particular person Himself. When I sense this is what the Holy Spirit is saying, I just quietly leave them to His ministry.

The prophetic is one of the ways that God communicates through His people, but God's heart is that everyone would hear Him directly and be able to recognise His voice for themselves. This is so important to God that He even set up prophets as part of the five-fold ministry to train and equip His body. God wants to be in a relationship with each one of us, so that He can communicate with His children.

The Way of Love

We must know the word of God to know God's will, purposes and intentions for our lives. We must understand who He is and what He is like so that we can represent Him well to others.

We are His ambassadors. There is no greater responsibility than to share the Gospel. Let us never take that privilege and honour lightly.

It is all about love.

I love that right in the middle of the gifts chapters in his letter to the Corinthians, Paul talks about the importance and central role of love. We must remember that the Kingdom of God is all about people and God loves people; they are His most treasured possession, most precious of all His creation. He shed His blood for people to save them.

So, when we operate in the prophetic gift, love must always be at the helm. We want to draw people closer to God, not drive them further away. We want them to be encouraged, to be lifted up, to be comforted, to have a chance to know our beautiful Creator the way that we do.

Above all else, this gift must operate out of love.

1 Corinthians 13:2-10, *'Though I speak with the tongues of men and of angels, but have not love, I have become sounding brass or a clanging cymbal. And though I have the gift of prophecy, and*

understand all mysteries and all knowledge, and though I have all faith, so that I could remove mountains, but have not love, I am nothing. And though I bestow all my goods to feed the poor, and though I give my body to be burned, but have not love, it profits me nothing. Love suffers long and is kind; love does not envy; love does not parade itself, is not puffed up; does not behave rudely, does not seek its own, is not provoked, thinks no evil; does not rejoice in iniquity, but rejoices in the truth; bears all things, believes all things, hopes all things, endures all things.

Love never fails. But whether there are prophecies, they will fail; whether there are tongues, they will cease; whether there is knowledge, it will vanish away. For we know in part, and we prophesy in part. But when that which is perfect has come, then that which is in part will be done away.'

Chapter 8

A Stranger's Voice We Will Not Follow

Chapter outline:

> - Discerning false prophecy and deceptive voices.
> - Strategies for testing the validity of prophetic words.
> - Safeguarding the prophetic ministry within the bounds of Biblical truth.

Counterfeit or True

How do we know what God's voice sounds like? As we discussed in Chapter 5, God's character and tone are reflected in His voice.

God's voice is not one that is:

Harsh

Offers no solution or help to the problems.

Criticising

Condemning

Unforgiving

Full of despair and full of hopelessness

Pushy
Legalistic
Destructive
Causes Doubt and Confusion
Unloving
Dishonouring
Controlling
Manipulating
Lording it over
"God said it therefore it is," taking away a person's ability to choose.
Angry
Discouraging
Bitter
Fearful
Anxious
Overbearing
Self-righteous

Our Plumb Line

We can receive great and amazing prophecies which are such a blessing and can help us in our walk with the Lord. But let us always remember to hang our lives on the perfect, infallible word of God.

The beloved Bible is a very clear plumb line that does not change or shift, one that we can trust with our whole lives.

The Bible gives us clear instructions about the gifts that are available to every believer and teaches us how to exercise them. It tells us that we are not to despise prophecy, but we are to always match them up with the word of God. God cannot and will not contradict His word. There is no more sure word of prophecy than the Bible – the testimony of Jesus Christ is the spirit of prophecy. The Bible is completely untainted by the filter of man. There is nothing that can be added or taken away from the word.

It is purified seven times and will never fail us, it is a light to our paths and a lamp unto our feet, it keeps us on the narrow path. I love that God's word does not change, there is no confusion or chaos, but clear and precise instructions. The Bible is not some cryptic puzzle we need to work out, as Scripture interprets Scripture. That is why we need to know the whole Bible, the goodness and the severity of God in its context, to get a whole picture of God's love letter to us.

The word of God is a powerful weapon, it is a two-edged sword! Not just a defence but also an offence. It cuts and it heals, it is designed to separate a lie from the truth.

2 Timothy 3:16 -17, *'All Scripture is given by inspiration of God and is profitable for doctrine, for reproof, for correction, for instruction in righteousness that the man of God may be perfect (mature) thoroughly furnished unto all good works.'*

Hebrews 4:12, *'For the word of God is living and powerful and sharper than any two-edged sword, piercing, even to the dividing apart of soul and spirit, and the joints and marrow, and is a discerner of the thoughts and intents of the heart.'*

God never goes against His word; He cannot. His word is forever settled in Heaven. He cannot change, He is the same yesterday, today and tomorrow. He is the solid rock on which we can stand; we can fully put our trust in Jesus.

I am so grateful and thankful for the precious word of God - a great light in gross darkness and the plumb line of our humanity. It shows us how to be spiritual, how to live out this life with the heart of God, what we are to do and what we are not to do, and where our choices will lead us. God maps it out so clearly for us from Genesis to Revelation. He is the Alpha and the Omega, the Beginning and the End.

I thank God for those who risked their lives, who were brutally martyred, so that we can have the Bible readily available today in every language. What a gift - something that we should treasure and never, ever take for granted.

No matter how our culture or society changes, no matter how far they try to move the measuring stick for morality, one thing that we can be sure of - God's word always remains the same. He does not change His mind, He has no darkness in Him, the rug will not be pulled out from underneath you. He loves you so much and He is trustworthy and faithful.

False Prophets and True Prophets — how do we tell the difference?

Jeremiah 23:16-18, *'Thus says the Lord of hosts: "Do not listen to the words of the prophets who prophesy to you. They make you worthless; They speak a vision of their own heart,*
Not from the mouth of the Lord. They continually say to those who despise Me,
'The Lord has said, "You shall have peace"';
And to everyone who walks according to the dictates of his own heart, they say,
'No evil shall come upon you.'"
For who has stood in the counsel of the Lord, And has perceived and heard His word?
Who has marked His word and heard it?'

Matthew 7:15, *'Beware of false prophets, which come to you in sheep's clothing, but inwardly they are ravenous wolves.'*

Matthew 24:11-12, *'And many false prophets shall rise, and shall deceive many. And because iniquity shall abound, the love of many shall wax cold.'*

Matthew 24:24, *'For there shall arise false Christs, and false prophets, and shall shew great signs and wonders; insomuch that, if it were possible, they shall deceive the very elect.'*

Luke 6:26, *'Woe unto you, when all men shall speak well of you! For so did their fathers to the false prophets.'*

2 Peter 2:1, *'But there were false prophets also among the people, even as there shall be false teachers among you, who privily shall bring in damnable heresies, even denying the Lord that bought them, and bring upon themselves swift destruction.'*

1 John 4:1, *'Beloved, believe not every spirit, but try the spirits whether they are of God: because many false prophets are gone out into the world.'*

True and False prophets according to Jeremiah 23:21-22, *'I have not sent these prophets, yet they ran: I have not spoken to them, yet they prophesied. But if they had stood in my counsel, and had caused my people to hear my words, then they should have turned them from their evil way, and from the evil of their doings.'*

> True prophets:
> Speak God's word faithfully.
> Draw people to Jesus Christ not themselves.
> Never water down the message
> Confront sinful cultures and idols of the day.
> Have fierce love and respect for the word of God.
> Tried and tested in character.
> Integral, honest, pure, holy
> Turn people back to the truth.
> Warn of the coming judgement.
> Preach repentance and remission of sins.
> Turn people away from wickedness.
> Stand in the counsel of God.
> Have a heart for true justice.
> Love people enough to tell them the truth.

Understand the goodness and severity of the Lord.
Submitted and accountable to church Authority
Work in conjunction with the body of Christ.
Cause people to hear God's word.
Build, plant, and establish God's word in people's lives.

True prophets are recognised for their love and ability to hear the Father's heart of God for people.

False prophets:
Strengthen the hands of evildoers.
Prophesy for fame/gain.
Compromise the word of God.
Are liars.
Masquerade as an angel of light.
Love the praises of man.
Are ravening wolves in sheep's clothing.
Lone rangers, not submitted to Authority.
Not accountable to anyone
Draw people to themselves and their gifting.
Say 'peace, peace where there is no peace'.
Say, 'No evil shall come upon you.'
Share the visions of their own hearts.
Cause people to err by perverting God's word.
Cause people to forget God's name.
Call the way of truth evil.

The Greek word for 'false prophet' is 'psyoo-dace', from Strong's number G5574; untrue, that is, erroneous, deceitful, wicked: - false, liar.

Test All Things

The Bible shows us clearly in the end days many false prophets and teachers will arise, deceiving many! TEST ALL THINGS!!!

2 Peter 2:1-3 (KJV), *'But there were false prophets also among the people, even as there shall be false teachers among you, who privily shall bring in damnable heresies, even denying the Lord that bought them, and bring upon themselves swift destruction.*

And many (imitate, obey, yield) shall follow their pernicious ways; by reason of whom the way of truth shall be evil spoken of.

And through covetousness (extortion, fraudulency, greediness) shall they with feigned (artificial, moulded, fictitious) words make merchandise (peddler, travel in, peddler, buy and sell) of you: whose judgment now of a long time lingereth not, and their damnation slumbereth not.'

It says here there will be "many" (imitate, obey, yield) false prophets and teachers arising in the last days. We are already seeing this rapid increase through the medium of the internet. We are seeing pop-up ministries all over Facebook, people that may not even be properly qualified or ordained as ministers. Most of them are lone rangers and are not involved in a local church or working within the ordained leadership of a church. They usually have little or no background in ministry, and most of the time their character has not been tried and tested. These people have usually been offended by the church or have just stepped out on their own.

We see the motive of a false prophet's heart is greed, the love of money. Money is not evil in itself, but it is the love of money that is the root of all evil. They are fraudulent and deliberately deceive people with false, artificial words for monetary gain.

1 John 4:1, *'Beloved, believe not every spirit, but try (prove, test, allow, discern, examine) the spirits whether they are of God: be-*

cause many false prophets (pretender, foreteller) are gone out into the world.'

Again, I encourage you to test all things! The Bible says to test all things, do not just believe everything you hear; always take it and compare it to the word of God.

1 Thessalonians 5:21, *'Prove all things; hold fast that which is good.'*

Activation

How do we test a prophetic word?
Think of a prophetic word you have received or given recently.
Here are some filters it needs to go through:

- Does it line up with the word of God?
- Does line up with the heart and character of God?
- Is it leading me closer to God and His purposes, or further away?
- Is it confirmation of what you are thinking, feeling or of another prophetic word you have previously received?
- Is it edifying, comforting, or exhorting?

Chapter 9

Calling Things That Are Not As Though They Are

Chapter outline:

> - Exploring the prophetic act of speaking life into situations.
> - Biblical examples of speaking prophetically to change circumstances.
> - Testimony - encouragement to exercise faith and declare God's promises through prophecy.

Prophesy to Those Bones!

God speaks to us and reminds us that it does not matter what things look like in our natural circumstances, WE can call those things that are NOT, as thou they ARE.

In the book of Ezekiel, we are given a powerful example of just how we can do this.

Ezekiel 37:1-5, *'The hand of the Lord came upon me and brought me out in the Spirit of the Lord and set me down in the midst of the valley; and it was full of bones. Then He caused me to pass by them all around, and behold, there were very many in the open valley; and indeed, they were very dry. And He said to me, "Son of man, can these bones live?" So, I answered, "O Lord God, You know."*

Again, He said to me, "Prophesy to these bones, and say to them, 'O dry bones, hear the word of the Lord! Thus says the Lord God to these bones: "Surely I will cause breath to enter into you, and you shall live.'

God gives Ezekiel a vision of a valley full of very dry bones and He challenges Ezekiel and asks him, "Son of man, can these bones live?"

Ezekiel's great response is, "O Lord God, You know."

Again, God says to Ezekiel, *"Prophesy to these bones and SAY to THEM, 'O dry bones hear the Word of the Lord.'"* Everything on this earth, in Heaven and under the earth recognises and responds to God's word accordingly. The wind and the waves obeyed Jesus then, and they obey Him now. Jesus has been given all authority and the same Spirit that raised Jesus Christ from the dead lives in us.

God is teaching Ezekiel through His relationship with him, how to SPEAK to those dead situations, those situations that look like they have no life, those nations and cities that in the natural look like things are hopeless. There are many who are trapped in sin and hopelessness and apathy, and it is up to us to SPEAK and partner with God's plan over their lives.

'So, I prophesied as I was commanded, and as I prophesied there was a noise and suddenly a rattling and the bones came together, bone to bone. Indeed, as I looked the sinews, and the flesh came

upon them, and the skin covered them over but there was no breath in them.' (Ezekiel 37:7-8).

Situations are just waiting for you to speak to them to live in Jesus' name.

'Also, He said to me, "Prophesy to the breath, prophesy, son of man, and say to the breath, 'Thus says the Lord God: "Come from the four winds, O breath, and breathe on these slain, that they may live."'" So, I prophesied as He commanded me, and breath came into them, and they lived, and stood upon their feet, an exceedingly great army."' (Ezekiel 37:9-10)

There are many valleys of dry bones, many nations where it looks impossible for God to be able to take the nation back; the churches look dead and only two percent of the population are Christians. Let me tell you - start to prophesy life into that ground! There are armies of the Lord just waiting for you to SPEAK life over dead and dry bones. Many people give up after they see a little bit of movement, but you need to keep prophesying as God commands. He has already sent the commands out; we prophesy according to His will and His character.

We must begin to speak into situations until you see those things that are not, as thou they are.

In Jesus Christ God has already given us FULL authority to bring Heaven to earth, but for it to do any good and bring any change we must understand we need to use it; we need to be doers of His word. In the prophetic you need to be like a dog with a bone and contend to see God's Kingdom established here on earth.

There is an excellent story in the Bible that illustrates how we need to contend for God's will to be done. We contend in faith because we hear prophetically what God is doing or has already done in the life of a person, a city or a nation.

1 Kings 18:1, *'And it came to pass after many days that the word of the Lord came to Elijah, in the third year, saying, "Go, present yourself to Ahab, and I will send rain on the earth."*

Elijah goes to King Ahab and in faith, because of the word of the Lord, says to him, *"Go Up eat and drink, for there is the sound of the abundance of rain"* (1 Kings 18:41)

Verse 42-44a, *'So, Ahab went up to eat and drink. And Elijah went up to the top of Mount Carmel, then he bowed down on the ground and put his face between his knees and said to his servant "Go up NOW and LOOK towards the sea" He went up and looked* (here we see obedience) *and said, "There is NOTHING" and seven times he said, "GO AGAIN" and then it came to pass the seventh time...'*

So, let us just stop here for a moment and imagine this scenario from the servant's perspective: you have been given the word of the Lord by your leader. You know what He has told you to do, and six times you have physically looked into the sky (six times you have been obedient). In the natural what you see six times is a cloudless sky. I mean, would you not be thinking at this point, "Umm ... Elijah, I am not sure if this is working. There is not a cloud in the sky and there has not been a single cloud every time I have looked." Yet, a prophetic person calls those things that are not, as though they are. The prophetic sees beyond the natural circumstances, beyond what can only be seen with our physical eyes.

Many times, I have prophesied things that would happen as God has shown me, when it looked impossible in the current circumstances. In fact, the current circumstances looked the exact opposite of what God was showing me.

Let us continue with this Scripture, *'He said," there is a cloud, as small as a man's hand rising out of the sea!" So, he said "Go up to Ahab, prepare your chariot, and go down before the rain stops you."*

Now it happened in the meantime that the sky became black with clouds and wind, and there was a heavy rain. So, Ahab rode away and went to Jezreel. Then the hand of the Lord Elijah and he girded up his loins and ran ahead of Ahab to the entrance of Jezreel.' (1 Kings 37:44b-46)

We have to be relentless in our pursuit to see the Kingdom of Heaven established on the Earth. We can have the word of the Lord, but we also need to couple that with obedience and patience to see it fully come to pass. We simply cannot afford to look at the natural circumstances and be discouraged and think God is not moving. We have to understand and have a resolve in our hearts to believe that there is NO IMPOSSIBLE situation for God to move in. When we partner with God and co-labour with His will for the Earth, ALL things are possible. Only believe and YOU WILL SEE the Glory of God.

The Power of Life and Death is in the Tongue.

Jeremiah 1:9-10, *'Behold I have put my words in your mouth, see I have this day set YOU over the NATIONS and OVER the KINGDOMS, to ROOT OUT, and to PULL DOWN, to DESTROY and to THROW DOWN, to BUILD and to PLANT.'* (emphasis added)

God wants us to SPEAK into situations where there is darkness and destroy and demolish darkness everywhere we go. We do not need to ask Him to do it, instead we need to understand that He is asking us to speak.

'Death and life are in the power of the tongue, And those who love it will eat its fruit.' (Proverbs 18:21)

God gave me a dream and in that dream there was a husband and wife telling me about the change they saw in their son after I had prophesied over his life. I was listening to what they were saying and just began to weep in the dream. I was weeping over this man's life and then, as I was doing that, God showed me this young man's bedroom and what was happening in the spirit once the word of the Lord goes out: I saw dead branches everywhere, vines and plants in his room that were dead. The leaves were crispy and brown; I mean very dead, every part of the plant, the stem as well. In the dream, as the word of the Lord, words of life and life more abundantly, were spoken over this young man's life, I began to see life come back into the dead plants in the young man's room. Slowly the stems started to turn green, bit by bit. The vines started to come alive again bit by bit, and I began to watch life fill every stem, every branch, every leaf, until the room was full of life again, flourishing, and bright and vibrant.

This is beautiful picture of the heart of Heaven for humanity.

God wants us to see people through the eyes of Jesus. He wants us to ask God what the purposes and plans are that He had in mind when He created the person standing in front of you. There are always problems and different issues in people's lives, some more glaringly obvious than others, but the prophetic should offer solutions to our problems, a way out, a loving Father ready to receive a repentant son or daughter. A prophetic word is a calling back of people - back to the words of God, back to the way, back to the truth and back to the life of God. To turn their hearts back to the only wise and living God. This is God's restorative, reconciling character reflected in His voice.

We are to invite the person to see God's plans and purposes for their life, to reveal God's heart to them in a personal and intimate way.

My life is a good example of what I mean by calling those things that are not, as though they are. I was a raging alcoholic, a hard-hearted atheist, but I had a radical encounter with God and sorely repented. I was born again, and everything changed.

Even before my life began on the earth, God had a plan and purpose for my life. His vision for my life was to be a minister of the Gospel. He knew the enormous potential I had, even though I could not see it and there was absolutely no shred of evidence of this master plan evident in my life. I was neck-deep in sin and transgressions and was rapidly drowning.

In fact, every circumstance in my life was screaming the exact opposite – I was surrounded by chaos and destruction and brokenness at every turn. I was not living; I was merely existing. I was constantly and mercilessly tormented by lying demons who were trying desperately to take me down to the pit.

I would have laughed my head off if someone had told me that I would be a minister, overseeing churches with my husband and four children. At the time, I was a single mum with one child, having had one failed relationship after another, and absolutely hated Christianity. None of God's plans and purposes for my life were even remotely present in my world back then. I would not have believed them for a second.

Here is the thing - I was living in the wrong identity, and I was in total darkness. I was living as an enemy of the cross being shaped into the wrong person by the enemy. Being discipled by demons of death, the identity of darkness was my story. But God had a different plan, one of hope and restoration, one of healing and mercy. He transferred me out of the kingdom of darkness and into His glorious light. He had a destiny and a plan for my life all along.

There are so many precious people who are living in the wrong identity. We want to call out in them what God sees and what God created them for – their true identity.

When we prophesy God's words according to the Bible and His character, they are words of life, living and active. You are pouring hope upon them and giving people an opportunity to respond to what God wants to do. We are giving people an opportunity to step into something greater than what or where they are. It offers them a different path than the one they are currently on. It gives them a path of grace to get back on the right path if they have strayed. It is their choice to accept the invitation or not. God will not force anyone to follow Him; He will encourage us to do so, but He has gifted us with a free will.

His Bride

I want to say a few words about how we can speak life into the Church as a whole, the Bride of Christ. So many are ready to tear down the Church with all its problems and imperfections. I understand that there are some specific things that need to be realigned with God's word. But overall God says clearly that we are to edify the Church. The Church is very important to God, it is His Bride, and He gave His precious, only begotten Son for her.

Instead of using our words to tear down the Church and focus on what she is not, let us speak by faith and speak about who she is and is destined to become.

The power of life and death is in the power of the tongue we must continue to speak life, hope, mercy, truth, and love.

Activation

Is there a situation/circumstance in your life or in the life of a friend or family member that needs life spoken into it?

Is there a dream or a plan that has been lying dormant in your heart for a long time?

Is there depression or discerned oppression lying like a wet blanket over your life or the life of a loved one?

Ask God what He wants you to speak over those things? What would He say to bring life to those dead things? What would He have you say to those things that are not, as though they are?

Imagine those things moving and full of life.

Now speak those things God gives you over those dead bones!

Chapter 10

Stepping Out To Prophesy

Chapter outline:

> - Overcoming fear and hesitation to release prophetic words
> - Practical steps to develop and mature in the prophetic
> - The role of mentorship and accountability in prophetic growth
> - Nurturing a lifestyle of intimacy with God to enhance prophetic sensitivity
> - Practical exercises for stepping out in faith
> - How to give and receive prophetic words with wisdom and maturity

A Good Place to Start

It can seem daunting when you first step out in the prophetic gift, but if you keep the words you speak, as the Bible tells us, to be edifying, to build up and bring comfort, honestly you can't go wrong.

When I first became a Christian, I had a crippling fear of speaking in front of people and would start to shake the moment I stood up to speak. I remember being asked to bring a communion message in a church service. The mere thought of presenting a message for the church in front of people made me feel physically ill. I just could not do it. Then I got asked about six months later to share my testimony, so I wrote it down and read it off the piece of paper. My hands were shaking so badly I could not even have a sip of water as it would have spilt, for sure. Despite my fear, there was not a dry eye in the church and the Holy Spirit rocked the place; so many people were set free. I had made no eye contact with anyone and was definitely not an eloquent speaker, but was instead a very scared little girl, way out of my depth, cowering behind the pulpit.

We all have to start somewhere, and fear is something that we all have to overcome by pushing ourselves and believing what the Word says about us, *'The wicked flee when no one pursues, But the righteous are bold as a lion.'* (Proverbs 28:1)

That's right, you read it correctly, the righteous ARE, not going to be bold but already ARE, as bold as lions.

A good place to practice the prophetic is in a home group setting where there are not as many people, and it is a safe environment. The more you exercise this gift the easier it gets. Step out whenever you have an opportunity - when you feel like it and when you do not.

The enemy would love for you to get discouraged and stop stepping out in the gift, but we need to keep persevering. It is a gift that needs to be exercised. Let's use the gym as an example - when we first start off at the gym, it is hard and awkward, it seems really difficult and uncomfortable, but if you go consistently a few times and get used to the new process, it becomes easier and easier. Like anything new in life, you may feel discouraged at times, but that is not the time to give up. No-one starts off being excellent at what they do. They end up being excellent by not giving up, by persevering, and eventually they see the fruit of their labour.

When I first started giving people words of knowledge, I got the details wrong many times, but as I kept stepping out and persevering, I began to hear with more and more clarity.

While you are growing and learning, it is okay to get words of knowledge wrong. Keep trying. Just step out and have a go. God is rapt when we step out of our comfort zones.

When I first started, I began by seeking words for people during the week: I would ask God to highlight a Scripture that would help them and encourage them.

I would write words down for people and give it to them in a card or text them. They were greatly encouraged, and I could see the huge difference it was making to their walk with God - it drew them closer to Him.

How Do I Grow in the Prophetic?

The best way to get better at anything is to practice and practice. Do not get discouraged if you mess it up. Be gracious to yourself as you learn to hear God's voice. The enemy wants to discourage you and make you feel embarrassed; he wants to stop you from sharing what God really thinks about people.

God is always wanting to communicate with people, He wants them to know He is real and the prophetic is powerful and changes lives. I know - it completely changed mine.

The goal is not to just give people a prophetic encouragement but to introduce them to Jesus, to let them know that it is Jesus Who knows their situation. That He hears and He sees them; we cannot know that information in the natural; it is a supernatural gift.

If you are struggling with fear, here are some simple ways that I learnt to step out in the prophetic:

- If you are out for dinner, for instance, write a prophetic word on a serviette for the waiter or the waitress.
- When you are out shopping, ask someone if they would like a word of encouragement, or
- Ask someone if you can take their trolley back for them and tell them about the love of God.
- Ask people, "Do you have any prayer needs that I can pray for?" As you start praying, the prophetic will start to flow. As you pray, you might only have one word or a simple picture of, for example, a flower, but it can mean the world to someone.

I just say to God, "Just tell me one thing about that person so that they will know that You are real."

Ask the person you are prophesying over if it resonates with them; it is important to get feedback because sometimes we might get just one detail the Lord has shown us, but upon speaking to the person that picture becomes so much clearer.

It is important that we know whether we are hearing from God or not. All feedback is valuable, so do not get discouraged if the word you gave them was not right or didn't resonate with the person. You will learn, you will grow, you will get stronger and more accurate.

Sometimes you will have just one word, but unbeknown to you God may have been highlighting that one word to them all week. We cannot know that in the natural, but God knows because He sees and know everything we are doing. You do not need to add or take away from what He is saying. Just speak, plain and simple, and watch how He will move through a faithful vessel.

Sometimes what you share with someone could be the difference between life and death for them. I have encouraged so many people not knowing that they were planning to take their life. The enemy is terrorising all of humanity to try and kill, steal, and destroy people. Our wonderful mandate is to bring life where there is death, hope where there is hopelessness and beauty for ashes. We want to transform lives by bringing Heaven to earth. We overcome evil with GOOD!!

Seeing the broken nursed back to life, seeing people transformed by the Gospel is the greatest miracle in the world, because only God can change a hardened heart, only God's Spirit can bring the dead things back to life.

Start using the gift wherever you are; look for people who you can bless and encourage with the gift on your life. God does not want us to hoard it for ourselves, but rather to share it so that others can be blessed and grow.

I would look for people in my life at church and just send them a card with some words of encouragement, or send a text or call them, just to bring refreshment from the Lord. It is amazing! Everyone needs encouragement. In fact, the Bible says to exhort (encourage) one another daily as the day of the Lord approaches. You cannot use this gift enough. Building people up is such a wonderful thing to do and it really blesses God's heart to see His body loving on each other and strengthening and getting alongside one another in the hard times as well as the good.

Never give up sharing the love of God we must be the light in great darkness. The enemy is working in overdrive to torment people in this world by telling them who they are not, and how they will never measure up and never be good enough.

God does not tell us who or what we are not, but He reminds us of who we truly are. He reminds us that we are His beloved treasure in earthen vessels and that He wants to partner with us to get His work done here on this earth.

We are responsible to share the word God gives us, however, we are not in any way responsible for the way that people react or do not react to His word. That is between them and God.

We bring the seed of the word of God, and we plant and water as much as we can, but we must remember that it is God who brings the increase. Do not be discouraged if you do not see a harvest in front of your eyes, because God will continue to breathe upon His word that you spoke, until it bears fruit.

'So then neither he who plants is anything, nor he who waters, but God who gives the increase.' (1 Corinthians 3:7)

Also, do not get discouraged by peoples' reactions to the words you give them. There have been some amusing times when, after receiving a word of knowledge for someone, they would get so startled that I knew something about them that they would deny it and take off! They would, however, come back later and say it was true, they just did not want to acknowledge it.

The Bible tells us that none of God's words will come back to Him void but will accomplish all that which it has been sent to do.

'So shall My word be that goes forth from My mouth;
It shall not return to Me void,
But it shall accomplish what I please,
And it shall prosper in the thing for which I sent it.' (Isaiah 55:11)

Practical steps and activities

When was the last time you stepped out and gave a word?

Think of three people right now and ask God for a word for them and text it to them or write it down.

When I am with someone who is wanting prayer, I will ask God, "What is happening in this person's life currently? What do you dream over their life? How do you want to encourage them today, Lord?"

And then I wait for His response; He may show me a simple picture, give me a Scripture verse, use an analogy, give me a song to sing over them - always speaking hope and life, which is refreshing for the weary and broken. Hope is the anchor of the Gospel; we all need hope and all need to hold onto hope. It is what sees us through the hard times and helps us see the light at the end of the tunnel, that our circumstances aren't at a dead end, but there is breakthrough right around the corner. Hope encourages us and helps us to keep going. When people understand that God sees and hears them, it refreshes hope and vision and purpose in their lives, regardless of where they are. We always want to draw them one step closer to King Jesus with this gift.

After I have prophesied, I will ask them, "Does that make sense to you?"

As I said earlier, it is important to get feedback to help us grow in giving prophetic words. Sometimes God will just give you a small piece of what is going on, but when you ask for feedback, the person will share in greater detail.

The Miner with a Pickaxe

I once hosted a home group in my house, and there was a very sceptical gentleman who started attending. At this point, he did not understand how God would personally talk to me. He did not believe in healing, and we had many debates over the Scriptures.

One night, each person in the group had to draw someone's name out of a hat and then we had to give that person a prophetic word the next week.

Of course, I got the sceptical gentleman's name and fear gripped me that whole week! I had dreaded getting this man's name, but I knew that God wanted to teach me something, as He always does! So, I said to God, "You need to provide me with something accurate and true that I can't possibly know."

Well, God is so faithful. As I prayed and waited on God, He gave me a picture of a gold statue of a miner with a pickaxe. God was showing me in pictures, and this is what I saw:

I saw a picture of this man with a pickaxe trying to find gold in caverns and mines, and he got frustrated and threw the pickaxe down. Then I saw caverns of gold and him laughing with joy and freedom. God showed me that the pickaxe represented religion.

Well, I hoped the whole week that this man wouldn't turn up so that I did not have to share this weird word with him, which made absolutely no sense to my mind. The thought of him jeering and laughing at God was more than I could handle. Well, he was the first to turn up! The time came for us to pass our words on. I waited until the end of the night to give my piece of paper to the gentleman, so that I did not have to see him read it.

Well, the very next day I got a phone call from him: "I want to talk to you about the word you gave me." I gulped. This was the moment I had been dreading. I praise God that I have been delivered from fear, but back then, I was feeling and experiencing the anxiety something fierce!

He goes on to tell me how he does not like those dust-cluttering ornaments everyone has in their homes and how much they annoy him. I gulp, then he tells me, "But I have just one, which someone gave me, which I have kept. It is near my bed, and it's a gold statue of a miner with a pickaxe in his hand." He continues to tell me, "You don't know this, but I was born and brought up in a gold mining town." To say I felt relieved was an understatement. I sighed the biggest relief ever in my life!

This sceptical gentleman started to cry and said, "You do hear God talk to you!" We did not debate anymore after that. He was a sceptic no more and he began to leave his old religious beliefs behind, and he fell in love with Jesus. I watched an incredible relationship form between him and God. He would weep in the presence of the Holy Spirit. God started to change His heart through one word given to him by a terrified baby Christian.
We ended up being great friends.

God wants us all to be able to prophesy and we all can; we can all be hope-bringers to a lost and dying world.

Words to Ponder

Sometimes God will give you a word for someone which is not meant to be released yet. We need to know when to speak out a word we have received, and when to hold it in our hearts. Sometimes God will show me something that is six years away from happening. So, understanding God's timing is crucial.

Just like Mary the mother of Jesus in Luke 2:19, *'But Mary kept all these things and pondered them in her heart.'* We need to sometimes ponder things in our hearts.

Sometimes God has shown me things that He just wants me to pray over and see a situation turn around. Always ask God, "Do you want me to share this at this time?"

At other times will, God will sometimes just tell you things about how your day is going to go, or not go, like when He told me about the roadworks, just so that you can learn to know His voice - what is of Him and what is not. It is all valuable information.

Giving and Receiving Words

When you are first learning, it is best to stay away from directional words, like for example, who a person is going to marry, when they are going to have a baby, and so on. Those words can be really damaging to a young believer, especially if they are not accurate.

I am not saying never give these kinds of words, because I know from experience that God would give me words like this constantly. Very early on in my prophetic journey, I remember a couple in church for whom it was physically impossible to have children. It had been medically diagnosed and it could not happen.

Every time I went to pray for them, I would see them with a baby boy in a pram. I saw this numerous times. I was a young believer at this point, so I took it to my pastors, and they gave me permission to share this word with the couple. So, I told them what I saw. They were initially offended as they had asked God for a girl. She did indeed fall pregnant, and they didn't tell anyone the gender of the baby until they walked into church one day, and sure enough, they had a baby boy in a pram. To this day, they have not had any other children.

Praise God the word was right. If I had of got it wrong, it could have caused them a lot of unnecessary grief and torment. Always take those kinds of words to your pastor or team leaders, especially when you are first learning. Try to stick to simply giving people encouraging, edifying, and comforting words when you are first learning. You cannot go wrong with encouragement.

I will give you an example of how a directional word can go really wrong. Let us say the person you are prophesying over may already be feeling restless, and then you say, "I see God moving you to China." Because they are a young believer, they immediately start selling all their stuff, pack up and go within a few weeks. They drop everything that God is already doing in their lives in preparation for future missions.

They arrive in China full of zeal, full of passion, only to find that everything is a disaster. There are no open doors (they have tried to open doors in their own steam), they have little income as they have given up their jobs and pulled out all the stops to get there financially; they have left their family behind and sold their possessions. They are quickly realising that there is no grace for this mission at all. They last a little while, only to move back feeling defeated, humiliated, and disappointed and sometimes very bitter because they did what they thought God had told them to do. What they did not realise was that it may have been a correct word, but they needed to ask God about the timing. Maybe God was going to send them in ten years' time, once character and endurance had been formed in them, enough to handle the demonic attack that would try and come against them and their family.

As the person who gave them the prophetic word, you might say, "What happened? I thought it was God?" Perhaps what you saw was the truth, but timing is very important in the prophetic. Maybe you were truly sensing the word, but it was for ten or twenty years down the track. If you have one of those impressions for someone, always season it with wisdom. I would say to the person, "This is what I see. I am not sure of the timing. Please test this word, talk it over with your pastor, as this could be something for the future."

Here is another example of how immature Christians can receive your word the way it is not intended: you give a directional word like "I see a new relationship forming that God is saying 'yes' to." The person you are talking to is already married but is looking for a way out of their marriage. They mistakenly think that God is giving them permission to leave their marriage to pursue this new relationship. This is not what you said, but it is how they have perceived your word.

We need to be really clear when we give a prophetic word and not use ambiguous words that can be understood in a number of different ways. God will never go against His word. Under normal circumstances, God would not advocate divorce, He advocates solutions.

Receiving a word with maturity and wisdom

It is really important that we test the prophetic words we are given (we will explore this further in Chapter 12). Not every word we get is from God; it might be a good word, but it may not be from God. When we receive a directional word, we should wait and get some Godly wisdom and counsel around that word. We do not need to rush into anything, especially if it could mean a huge shift for you and your family. Prematurely moving can also potentially uproot what God is currently doing in your life.

Maturity and wisdom say:

- Do not uproot yourself from your geographical location based on one directional prophetic word.
- Wait on the Lord, fast and pray and wait for further confirmation. Do not be quick to jump ship and make rash decisions.
- Speak to your family, pastor, and leaders before making big decisions. Ask for their wisdom and input

about the situation, seeking their counsel with your heart positioned to receive from them. Proverbs 11:14, *'Where no counsel is, the people fall: but in the multitude of counsellors there is safety.'*
- Consider the timing of such a move (is it now or somewhere in the future?)
- Consider the financial implications - visas, passports, bonds, moving, changing jobs.
- Consider the cost before you go; the grass is not always greener on the other side. You will have challenges, trials, and afflictions no matter where you live.
- Look at the motivation of your heart for wanting to move and make sure it is not because of offence or disunity with the brethren.

God definitely moves people geographically, but it happens a lot less frequently than we think. God also wants and needs faithful, steadfast people who will stay at their post and finish the job at hand. He needs those who can endure and overcome even in challenging circumstances. God needs people who are continually committed to seeing His Kingdom flourish. God needs people who have the capacity to grow under pressure and not to cave in under it. He needs those who will let Him deeply develop their character, moulding them more into the likeness of Jesus Christ. Unfortunately, so many people start great and wonderful ministries and churches, not realising the cost and pressure of the reality of the day-to-day grind. Once the shine of the new ministry has worn off, which, let's be honest, usually happens pretty quickly, people quickly move on to the next best thing.

In Luke 14: 28-30, Jesus says to count the cost before you start building, *"For which of you, intending to build a tower, does not sit down first and count the cost, whether he has enough to finish it— lest, after he has laid the foundation, and is not able to finish, all who see it begin to mock him, saying, 'This man began to build and was not able to finish?'"*

So, sometimes we just need to check the motivation of our hearts.

God is not schizophrenic – He is not disordered or chaotic in His thinking or His communication.

People have approached Daniel and I countless times over the years saying, "God has told me to serve in this ministry." They are so excited and so full of zeal. Then, three weeks down the track they come to us saying, "God has told me to move." Then, after being in the new place, they say God had told them something else. No, God wants you to be planted so that you can flourish in the house of God. Every time you uproot yourself (and it is not God's instruction) you have to start your discipleship all over again. God will deal with those issues in your life no matter where you go; so often we want to run away, instead of just letting God mould and shape our character.

Sometimes it can be easier to uproot ourselves, wanting something fresh and new, than to stay and work on something that has lost its initial shine. Sometimes it is simply our restless flesh wanting a new adventure, instead of being committed to learning and growing in maturity; learning the lessons that God has for us in that season. Let me be clear, however, that staying does not apply to abusive situations; God does not condone abuse.

The grass is not greener on the other side. The grass is always greener where you intentionally water it. One thing I have learnt along the journey is that God is interested in developing our character much more than our comfort. Hard seasons are actually good for us, they strengthen and challenge us and shape us more into the image of Christ. So often we want to run from a hard season, but there is purpose in the pain. Hard seasons remind us of our desperate need for the Lord; we should never leave that place of desperately seeking Him and pursuing Him.

I am reminded of the words in James 1:2 *"My brethren, count it all joy when you fall into various trials,"*. I used to think James was nuts, but looking back I am very grateful for those hard seasons when I have grown closer to God through those tough times. It is true He really does work everything together for the good of those who love Him.

One thing I have learnt is that even if I hear the word of the Lord directionally, I will not do anything rash or make quick decisions. I am a very slow mover when it comes to moving geographically in the Kingdom. I see it as a set of traffic lights – if it is orange, it means I have doubts or reservations. In that case, even if I have heard from God, I will not go, I will wait. Unless the light is absolutely green, I will put that word on the shelf and will pray and fast about it. I will consider all the options and implications and then wait some more. We can be so quick to drop good things that we are already doing for the Lord, instead of seeking Him for His timing about a move He is talking to us about.

If you have done all these things, been found faithful and it has been confirmed through your pastor and family that it is indeed God's word, you can look forward to a wonderful new season. There will be so much grace and ease and provision from God to carry on the next part of your journey. Doors will open up easily as the word tells us in Isaiah 22:22, *'The key of the house of David, I will lay on his shoulder; So he shall open, and no one shall shut; And he shall shut, and no one shall open.'*

One more thing - if you are currently involved in any type of service or ministry, is it really important to not rush to the next thing without handing the baton over properly and honourably, so that the work can continue to flourish. Be sure to tie up all the loose ends of where you are serving, and finish with integrity.

Partnering with God

Make war with your prophetic words.

What does that mean? It means if you believe you have received a word from God, hold onto it, pray over it, read it, and write it down.

It is great to write down prophetic words as we need to partner with them. We need to have faith that, if it is from God, it will surely come to pass. Let me say this though, do not just wait and wait around for that word to come to pass. Put it on the shelf, but not out of sight, and keep running with the call of God on your life.

I have had words that God spoke to me sixteen years ago that I have just started to see beginning coming to pass. Imagine if I had just waited and waited around for them to come to pass immediately. I would have wasted sixteen years of advancing God's kingdom.

Walking it out

Usually, when God gives us a word, there is a process involved to walking it out.

The story of Joseph is a good example of this principle. God gave him a dream, but it didn't come to pass straight away. In fact, things went horribly wrong after this magnificent dream. His brothers got jealous and tried to kill him, he was falsely accused of sexual assault and thrown into prison. He faced trial after trial, testing after testing; the Bible says it was to prove the Lord's word. He endured thirteen years of the process of walking it out before he saw what God had shown him.

You see, God needed someone trustworthy, someone with wisdom, someone teachable and humble, someone with knowledge and understanding of how to lead a whole nation out of famine. God needed to raise up someone faithful and steadfast to save people from starving during the famine. We see the beautiful heart that Jospeh displayed toward his brothers, despite all the trials he had been through as a result of their treatment of him. He welcomed his family with open arms and wept on their shoulders. He understood it was all part of God's plan and consequently was not bitter and resentful. He used the favour he had with Pharoah and invited them all to live very generously on his land, even though they had done great evil to him. God does not want us to get discouraged or bitter in the process of our journey. Instead, He wants to refine us in the process, purifying our motives and character.

One thing I have learnt about God is that He is never in a hurry. He is a slow and very deliberate builder. God develops our character through the process; we just need to keep our heart focused on him. When we live with this focus, we can enjoy the journey, knowing that our calling is not a destination, but a journey which takes a lifetime.

Sometimes I have received a word from God and seen things six or seven years in advance. It did not make sense at the time, but it is revealed as I walk the journey and stay with the process, partnering with God.

No prophetic word will just come to pass without your co-operation. Prophetic words are conditional. God reveals to us the potential of where we could be, and we need to take a step of faith. All through the Bible there are conditional promises, where God says, "I will, if you ..." There is no point knowing the word if it is not mixed with faith. It is faith that pleases God.

Hebrews 11:6, *'But without faith it is impossible to please Him, for he who comes to God must believe that He is, and that He is a rewarder of those who diligently seek Him.'*

God does not just speak for the sake of it; He wants us to hear what He is saying and do it, or at least take steps in that general direction.

To give you an example, I have had numerous words about writing a book. It has been a repeated theme by many different, unrelated people saying the same thing, I know it is God talking to me, so I have two choices to make - I can either procrastinate, knowing that God wants me to write a book to help others, or I can say, "Okay God, let's put a plan in place to get the job done for you." So, I daily set myself the goal of spending a couple of hours of uninterrupted time to get this book written. It will not write itself! I need to partner with God in it.

I believe if I had not started the process, I would still be receiving the "God wants you to write a book," words. It is so easy to say, "I am going to ... one day ... when I get around to it ... when I have the time ..." There are so many things we continually put out off in our lives, but we must be intentional and obedient, even if we do not know how to, even if we do not have the resources or the skill. If God has asked you to do it, He will help you.

Prophetic words for future events

Some prophetic words I have had, have still not come to pass. I have seen glimpses of them, but not the fullness of the words. Do not get discouraged if you have not seen a prophetic word come to pass yet. Continue to believe that if it is a word from God, it will come to pass. Above all else, however, we must hang our lives on the Scriptures and the promises of God.

Sometimes, God will give you a word with a specific time frame for future events.

At the very start of 2021 I remember God calling our family to the Sunshine Coast, in Queensland, Australia.

At our last church service in Victoria, before we left, God said to me, "What I have done in ten years, I will do in two". I shared this word with the whole congregation.

Based on this word, I knew there would be a significant acceleration in what we were doing.

This word was about something in the future with a specific timeline and result.

At that time my husband and I had planted four Fire Churches in Victoria, Australia, and we were heading to Queensland to plant one church on the Sunshine Coast.

Shortly after moving to the Sunshine Coast, we held our first Interest meeting (a meeting to gauge how many people would be interested in joining our church) on the 12th of February 2021 at the Night Quarter Venue. We had 1000 registrations!

Fast forward to 22nd of August 2021 and we planted Sunshine Coast Fire Church.

Soon afterwards, the Night Quarter venue went bankrupt, so we quickly found another venue.

In the same week, we found a more permanent building for our Fire Church Family. It was very run down and tired looking, but we didn't have any other options at this point. We took on the building and it would take about another month to get it ready for opening. We had an incredible team who re-painted, retiled, transformed the gardens, and helped restore this building to its former glory.

On the 12th of February 2023 we were finally ready to open it to the public.

I did not think anything about that date until someone reminded me of the word God had spoken to me when we left Victoria: "What I have done in ten years, I will do in two.

At that point, we had eight churches – in the two years since planting Sunshine Coast Fire Church, we ended up overseeing/planting three more Fire Churches: one in Rockhampton, one in Gold Coast and one in Brisbane.

So, we had planted four churches in ten years in Victoria, and another four Churches in two years in Queensland. God had fulfilled the prophetic word He gave me to the day!! You can't make this stuff up!

Sometimes a prophetic word is given to you prior to a tough time. It will not make one hundred percent sense at the time, but when you are in that difficult time or season you will remember that word, and it will bring comfort to you. This was the case when my husband, Daniel, received a dream from God about our daughter Abigail before she was conceived, as I described in chapter two. In the middle of incredibly challenging circumstances, I was so incredibly grateful for the dream that assured us that everything would be okay in the end. What a great comfort that brought to Daniel and me.

I love how God pre-warns us of things to come. The Holy Spirit leads us into all truth - He reveals things to us that are in the future, to help us, to guide us and to keep us from falling into potholes on the journey.

So, sometimes you may have a word for someone that does not make total sense at the time, but then they may come back to you at a later time and say that word was true and brought much comfort in a really difficult time.

When you are prophesying, just remember to faithfully speak what God is saying in that moment. Make every effort to ensure it is God you are hearing – we don't want to just be making stuff up in our imaginations. It is a fearful thing to speak on behalf of God. We must remain sober and in awe of the great privilege and honour it is to have this gift given to us. Never take it for granted. Treasure it, guard it and keep your heart pure and simple.

Activation

Have you ever received a prophetic word that has not come to pass? Do you think, after reading this chapter, that it may be for the future? Why not you pull it out and, if you haven't already, write it down and put it in a safe place for future reference.

Write down all the Bible verses God has highlighted for you over the years. Declare them aloud over whatever people or circumstances they apply to.

Chapter 11

Testing A Prophetic Word

Chapter outline:

> - A guide on how to evaluate and validate prophetic words.
> - Criteria for assessing the reliability of a prophetic message.
> - Maintaining humility and openness to correction in prophetic ministry.

Test All Things

1 John 4:1, *'Beloved, believe not every spirit, but try (prove, test, allow, discern, examine) the spirits whether they are of God: because many false prophets (pretender, foreteller) are gone out into the world.'*

We are not to just blindly accept everything we see and hear and assume that it is God's Spirit. God tells us to test the spirits using the word of God. This is not so that we become critical or suspicious of everyone, but to simply line up what people are saying with the Scriptures and character of God.

2 Timothy 3:13-14 (KJV), *'But evil men and seducers shall wax worse and worse, deceiving, and being deceived. But continue thou in the things which thou hast learned and hast been assured of, knowing of whom thou hast learned them;'*

This is a word study on the words **deceived** and **seducers**:

deceived - *planao* - to roam from safety, truth, go astray, virtue, err, wander, be out of the way.
seducers - *go'-ace* – to wail, properly a wizard (one who mutters spells), imposter.

1 Timothy 1:12-13, *'And I thank Christ Jesus our Lord who has enabled me, because He counted me faithful, putting me into the ministry, although I was formerly a blasphemer, a persecutor, and an insolent man; but I obtained mercy because I did it ignorantly in unbelief.'*

Some people can be genuinely ignorant and deceived. Saul (later called Paul) is an example of this. He was killing and persecuting Christians, thinking he was doing God a great service. When he encountered Jesus, he was radically transformed, so much so that God even renamed him Paul and he ended up writing most of the New Testament. Before his encounter with Jesus, he did not even realise he was deceived and was deceiving others.

Some people, however, are like ravenous wolves who are pretending to be something they are not. They are disguised as sheep but are inwardly wicked and are intentionally and deliberately destroying God's people.

Despite all these warnings, God also gives us simple instructions - to continue in the things of God and to stay in the truth.

How do we test the spirits?

How do we know when it is the spirit of error or the Spirit truth?

Here are some of the ways that God shows us clearly in the Scriptures how to differentiate between truth and error.

1 John 4:2-6, *'By this you know the Spirit of God: Every spirit that confesses that Jesus Christ has come in the flesh is of God, and every spirit that does not confess that Jesus Christ has come in the flesh is not of God. And this is the spirit of the Antichrist, which you have heard was coming, and is now already in the world. You are of God, little children, and have overcome them, because He who is in you is greater than he who is in the world. They are of the world. Therefore, they speak as of the world, and the world hears them. We are of God. He who knows God hears us; he who is not of God does not hear us. By this we know the spirit of truth and the spirit of error.'*

To summarise, a Spirit of truth will:

- Acknowledge that Jesus Christ has come in the flesh (1 John 2:22)
- Practice righteousness (1 John 3:7)
- Love their brothers or sisters (1 John 3:10)
- Not practice sin (1 John 3:9)
- Abide in the doctrine of Christ (2 John 1:9)
- Abide in Him and He in us. (1 John 3:6)
- Walk like Jesus walked (1 John 2:6)

- Depart from iniquity (2 Timothy 2:19)
- Crucify the flesh with its affections and lusts (Galatians 5:24)
- Obey God's commandments as they are not grievous (1 John 2:4)
- Purify himself as He is pure (1 John 3:3)
- 'He that knows God hears us, he that is not of God will not hear us.'
- Whoever is born of God does not practice sin, he keeps himself (preserves himself).
- By their fruit you will know them (Matthew 12:33) (Galatians 5:22)

The spirit of error:

- Whoever does not practice righteousness is not of God.
- Practices sin - does not purify himself.
- He who does not love his brother is not of God.
- Does not display genuine love for brothers and sisters.
- Does not love God and does not keep His commandments; they are grievous to him.
- Does not believe that Jesus is the Christ.
- Does not abide in the doctrine of Christ — has not the Father and the Son.
- Does not do good, so is not from God.
- Will not hear us who are of God.

People have created so many blurred lines of what is truly of God and what is not. These Bible verses help us to clearly see the differences.

We must also remember that there is a difference between being wicked and weak. When we are first born again, we are called 'babes in Christ', which means we must learn and grow to maturity by the renewing of our minds. Salvation is a process of sanctification, so when someone is truly born again we should be able to see transformation in their life as they learn about their new identity in the Lord.

Activation

Have you ever discerned a spirit of error?

Have you ever had a feeling that something is not right whenever you are with a particular person?

Have you ever had a physical sensation/response in your body/mood change whenever you encounter a particular person or are in a particular place?

Have you doubted your feeling and just put it down to your mood?

Can you think of that person or place now?

Ask God what He wants you to do about your discernment of this spirit of error.

Chapter 12

The Office Of A Prophet

Chapter outline:

- Examining the distinction between the gift of prophecy and the office of a prophet.
- The role of prophets in the Church and the world.
- Insights into the accountability and responsibility of those in prophetic leadership positions.

Ephesians 4:11-13, *'And He himself gave some to be apostles, some prophets, some evangelists, and some pastors and teachers, for the equipping of the saints of the work of ministry, for the edifying of the body of Christ till we all come to the unity of the faith and the knowledge of the son of God, to a perfect man to the measure of the stature to the body of Christ.'*

I want to bring some simple clarity to the differences between being in the office of a five-fold ministry, i.e. prophets, apostles, teachers, pastors, and evangelists.

First, let us talk about the God ordained role of the five-fold office of the Prophet. This can either be a male or a female, God is no respecter of persons.

Notice, Jesus gave SOME, not all, as Prophets. The office of a Prophet is a specific grace and function. Such a person is given as a gift to the Body of Christ for:

The work of the ministry
Perfecting or maturing of the saints.
Edifying (building) the Body of Christ.

It is the prophet's job to stir up the whole Body and teach and train all the saints to be able to recognise and hear the voice of God for themselves.

We do not get to pick and choose who is in the five-fold ministry. It is ordained by God. Before we were even born, God knew our place in His body. God says in Jeremiah 1:5, *"Before I formed you in the womb I knew you; Before you were born I sanctified you; I ordained you a prophet to the nations."'*

The word tells us that He is the one who sets the members in place in His body as it pleases Him. It does not say as it pleases us.

1 Corinthians 12:18, *'But now God has set the members, each one of them, in the body just as He pleased.'*

We cannot just appoint ourselves into any of the five-fold offices. God alone gives those positions. God's word sends a strong message to not appoint ourselves to these positions.

Revelation 2:20, *'Nevertheless I have a few things against you, because you allow that woman Jezebel, who calls herself a prophetess, to teach and seduce My servants to commit sexual immorality and eat things sacrificed to idols.'*

If you feel you are called into the five-fold ministry, in other words you feel you are either a teacher, a pastor, a prophet, an apostle or an evangelist, then there is a process - the call must first be recognised by another ordained and recognised five-fold minister. That minister must know you personally in regard to character and maturity, which is of the upmost importance to walking in the fullness of the calling.

Many are called but few are chosen. Many of us are called to do many wonderful things for the Lord, but few really give themselves completely to the call. Few are willing to pay the price and to do what it takes to see the call fulfilled. We must be willing to fully yield our will to the Word of God so that He can shape and mould our characters into the likeness of Jesus.

2 Chronicles 16:9, *'For the eyes of the Lord run to and from throughout the whole earth, to show himself strong on behalf of those whose heart is loyal to him.'*

1 Timothy 5:22 warns us not to lay hands on a man (or woman) too quickly as they may fall to pride if their character hasn't been tested and proven. *'Do not lay hands on anyone hastily, nor share in other people's sins; keep yourself pure.'*

1 Timothy 3:1-13, *'This is a faithful saying if a man desires the position of a bishop (superintendent) he desires a good work. A bishop then must be blameless, the husband of one wife, temperate, sober minded, of good behaviour, hospitable, able to teach, not given to wine, not violent, not greedy for money but gentle not quarrelsome, not covetous, one who rules his owns house well, having his children in submission with all reverence(for if a man does not know how to rule his own house, how will he take care of the church of God) not a novice, (a young convert, newly planted) lest being puffed up with pride (self-conceit, higher minded) he fall into the same condemnation as the devil. Moreover, he must have a good testimony among those who are outside, lest he fall into reproach and the snare of the devil.'*

'Likewise, must the Deacons (Minister, servant) be grave (honest, honourable) not double tongued, not given to much wine, not greedy of filthy lucre, holding the mystery of the faith in a pure conscience. And let these also first be proved (tested, approved, examine, try) then let them use the office of a deacon (serve), Being found blameless (irreproachable, Unaccused). Even so must their wives be grave (honest) not slanderers, sober faithful in all things let the deacons be the husbands of one wife, ruling their children and their own houses well. For they that have used the office of a deacon well purchase themselves a good degree and great boldness in the faith which is in Christ Jesus.'

We can see the above verses give us an extensive personal morality checklist that a minister must be displaying inwardly and outwardly to be entrusted further with God's house.

1 Thessalonians 2:4, *'But as we were allowed (test, discern, examine) of God to be put in trust with the Gospel, even so we speak (preach, say, talk, tell) not as pleasing men, but God, which tries (proves, tests) our hearts.'*

Ordaining someone is not something that should ever be done lightly or prematurely. Elders and ministers are sought to pray and fast and to be in total agreement to release you into the five-fold office.

None of these five-fold offices are meant to stand alone. God did not call any of us to be lone rangers in His Kingdom, but rather to work in conjunction with each other, being submitted to authority, planted in the house of God, so that we can all flourish, committed to the work of the ministry together, in unity, in God's house.

The whole point of being a five-fold prophet is not to show how well you can hear God's voice, but rather to train and equip the saints for the work of the ministry. Prophets should be teaching others how to recognise, respond to, and obey God's voice. A prophet's job is never to draw people to themselves to become enamoured with their gift. A prophet's job is to always point people back to Jesus, back to the Word and character of God.

The Gifts Are Given Without Repentance

Romans 11:29 (KJV), *'For the gifts and calling of God are without repentance.'*

My walk with God has been an interesting one. I have always been able to flow in the prophetic although I would not have recognised it as that. I would have called it *deja vu* or some other non-Christian term. Throughout my life I have always just known things that I could not know in the natural. Once I was born again, that gift increased. The more time I spent reading the Bible and in prayer, the clearer I would hear from God.

It was not until 2017 that someone recognised the office of a prophet on my life.

Over the years, I have been planting churches and serving in every facet of running a church. I just kept saying 'Yes' to God and was happy to do whatever He needed me to do, whenever He needed me to do it, for as long as He needed me to do it, even if it meant cleaning the toilets. God says when we are faithful in the small things, He will give us more responsibility.

The prophetic is a gift freely given to me from God, and gifts do not require us to repent and be right with God. God has given each one of us a free will to choose whether we will serve Him with the gifts and callings or not. Anyone can flow in a gift; we see it all the time in the world. As a quick example of this we see true psychics clearly using prophetic giftings for the Kingdom of darkness. They are using the gift that God freely gave them to benefit and draw attention to themselves and away from Jesus Christ.

That is why being able to flow in the gifts, in signs, wonders and miracles, is not a good indicator that someone is in right standing with God. We can be living in flat out sin and still see people healed and ministered to. Why? Because God loves people, and His mercy and compassion will reach past our sins in order to see someone restored and reconciled to him. God will, however, deal with the person living in sin later.

People can be operating with the gifts God gave them, and still be in unrepentant sin. Someone who is not following God in word and prayer, and has fallen away from intimacy with the Lord, will see that gift greatly diminish and move away from the Spirit of God and they will start operating under a spirit of deception. Remember, the enemy masquerades as an angel of light. It is so important to not just see the demonstration of the gift, but to also look for the fruits of the Spirit (character) in the person's life. If you want to prophesy and hear Him clearly, you need to be spending lots of time with Him to cultivate a deep friendship.

Jesus says in Matthew 7:22-23 (KJV), *'Many will say to me in that day, Lord, Lord, have we not prophesied in thy name? And in thy name have cast out devils? And in thy name done many wonderful works? And then will I profess unto them, I never knew you: depart from me, ye that work iniquity.'*

These are very sobering words from Pastor Jesus, ones that we need to take heed of. God is not okay with His children living in unrepentant, habitual sin. The people in this passage saying, "Lord, Lord," are people in the church. They are aware of the gifts and can operate in them, but they have made a 'lord' who is okay with their sin. That is not the true Jesus of the Bible. We need to make sure that we are doing everything 'as unto the Lord', for the audience of One. Even when we continue to grow in accuracy in the prophetic gift, we must remember that our identity comes from Christ alone. We must guard our hearts diligently and pray that we resist the temptation of becoming prideful. Or self-righteousness – that somehow, we are better than the next guy. The Bible encourages us to esteem others higher than ourselves. God does not give us gifts to gloat in our own glory. They are given to us to help and serve others. We do not have anything that God has not given us. He exalts the humble and abases the proud.

This word 'many' in this passage is frightening. This Scripture lists some the gifts here that are clearly done by the power of the Holy Spirit, and yet Jesus says, "depart from me you who practice iniquity or sin." We must make sure that we let God shape and mould our characters, that we live in purity and holiness and live consecrated lives before the Lord.

God's grace always empowers us out of sin, it does not keep us there. It is not a light thing to be entrusted with the Gospel; let us make sure Jesus gets all the glory. He is worthy of it all!!

Notice in this passage in Matthew, the people who Jesus did not know are listing gifts. There is not one mention of anything relating to the fruits of the Spirit. These people are operating in the gifts but are living in unrepentant iniquity. This shows us that we need both the gifts and the fruit of the Spirit.

By their fruits you will know (recognise) them (false prophets).

Jesus says in Matthew 7:15-20, *"Beware of false prophets, who come to you in sheep's clothing, but inwardly they are ravenous wolves. You will know them by their fruits. Do men gather grapes from thornbushes or figs from thistles? Even so, every good tree bears good fruit, but a bad tree bears bad fruit. A good tree cannot bear bad fruit, nor can a bad tree bear good fruit. Every tree that does not bear good fruit is cut down and thrown into the fire. Therefore, by their fruits you will know them."*

So, let us be led by the Spirit so that we can bear the wonderful fruit of the Spirit as we operate in the gifts that God has so freely given us. Then we can look forward to Jesus saying, "Well done, good and faithful servant."

Galatians 5:18-24, *'But if you are led by the Spirit, you are not under the law. Now the works of the flesh are evident, which are: adultery, fornication, uncleanness, lewdness, idolatry, sorcery, hatred, contentions, jealousies, outbursts of wrath, selfish ambitions, dissensions, heresies, envy, murders, drunkenness, revelries, and the like; of which I tell you beforehand, just as I also told you in time past, that those who practice such things will not inherit the kingdom of God.*

But the fruit of the Spirit is love, joy, peace, long suffering, kindness, goodness, faithfulness, gentleness, self-control. Against such there is no law. And those who are Christ's have crucified the flesh with its passions and desires.'

Activation

Ask God if there are any areas in your life that you need to repent of, so that you can walk in purity and holiness before God.

Postscript

I hope this book has blessed you and has given you a broad overview of some of the different facets of operating in the gift of prophecy, as well as some of the challenges, and also pitfalls, to watch and look out for.

I pray that as you read this book you will be able to clearly hear the voice of your Beloved. May you encounter and know the deep loving kindness and greatness of the King.

I pray that many lives will be changed and transformed as you partner with Jesus and step out in great boldness in the gifts He has given you to advance His Kingdom.

Chelsea Hagen is an ordained Australian Christian Churches minister, a recognised prophet, and a member of the Australian prophetic council. Her journey is one of radical transformation, beginning in 2004 when she encountered Jesus in a way that completely changed her atheist heart. From that moment, she embarked on a passionate journey, alongside her husband, Daniel Hagen, planting eight Fire Churches, each a testament to the life-giving power of the Gospel.

Married since 2008 and blessed with four children, Chelsea and Daniel are a testament to the transformative power of faith and love.

As the founder and senior minister of Fire Church, Chelsea leads with an unwavering commitment to sharing the message of hope and redemption that she herself experienced.

www.ingramcontent.com/pod-product-compliance
Lightning Source LLC
Chambersburg PA
CBHW062039290426
44109CB00026B/2668